Carving Fish Decoys

Carving Fish Decoys

A Traditional American Folk Art

James T. Cottle

Stackpole Books

Published by
STACKPOLE BOOKS
Cameron and Kelker Streets
P.O. Box 1831
Harrisburg, PA 17105

Printed in the United States of America

10 9 8 7 6 5 4 3 2 1

First Edition

A version of Chapter 1 appeared in *Michigan Out-of-Doors*, February 1990. It
was entitled "Pike Spearing Magic" and is reprinted here with permission of the
editor, Kenneth Lowe.

Photos and drawings by Stefan Cottle unless otherwise noted.

Library of Congress Cataloging-in-Publication Data

Cottle, James T.
    Carving fish decoys / James T. Cottle. — 1st ed.
        p. cm.
    Includes bibliographical references.
    ISBN 0-8117-1017-3
    1. Fish decoys. I. Title.
TT199.75.C68 1991
745.593'6 — dc20
                                         90-42858

To Celia and Clarence

Contents

Acknowledgments

I would like to thank Edeltraud Cottle, Anne DeFelice, Marie DiManno of the Museum of American Folk Art, Ron Edgerly, Art Kimball, James McKiddie, Rick Ojala, Angus Phillips, John Piper, and Mark Valesey for the assistance and encouragement you provided along the way to completion of this project.

Thanks also to Joanne Gigliotti of the Smithsonian Resident Associate Program and the Smithsonian Institution for arranging the courses and seminars on contemporary fish decoy carving. And a special thank-you to the students in these classes: your many comments, questions, and suggestions make it easier for those who follow you.

Foreword

The making of decoys for spearfishing is part of a long and rich tradition of ice fishing. There is documentary evidence that Native Americans have speared fish through the ice using handmade fish decoys since prehistoric times. The earliest decoys known are from around 1000 A.D. Since that time a wide variety of Native American handmade decoys have been found, particularly in the Great Lakes area. This utilitarian practice of ice fishing clearly has undergone a dramatic transformation over the past centuries. It has evolved from a subsistence practice of native peoples to a regional recreational activity that is a passionate cultural practice of ice fishermen while the ice is hard still today.

Carving Fish Decoys by James T. Cottle provides an overview of the history of ice fishing based on his own participation in traditional ice fishing in Sault Ste. Marie, Michigan. An avid spear fisherman and an accomplished maker of decoys, Cottle has a deep respect for the cultural life that surrounds the practice of ice fishing in communities throughout Michigan, Minnesota, and Wisconsin. Decoys do indeed vary from community to community and region to region. Most decoys were created for personal use or for friends and neighbors—not for wide circulation and sale. Hence, these practical creations reflect personal and local aesthetics.

This volume serves as a guide to those who want to create their own decoys. While it does provide carefully prepared and easy-to-follow directions, it encourages personal creativity. A true student of traditional ice fishing practices, Jim Cottle explains the subtleties he has learned from other ice fishing decoy carvers and his own scholarship. Beyond giving instructions for making decoys, the book also includes a guide to tools and equipment, a helpful list of supply sources, and a general bibliography.

Carving Fish Decoys offers the reader a fine practical guide to the making of decoys that will inspire carvers not only to make their own fish decoys but also to respect the practice of ice fishing as an American living tradition.

C. Kurt Dewhurst, Ph.D.
Director
Michigan State University Museum

Introduction

Fish decoys are first and foremost functional objects used to attract large fish, primarily pike and muskies, for the purpose of spearing them through a hole in the ice.

Since this function is of primary importance, even the beginning carver can successfully complete a decoy on the first attempt as long as the placement of the weight and hardware is correct. There is no need to worry about whether the carving looks exactly like a real fish or other prey for pike or musky. More important is its action. Does it swim properly? That's the key.

If one takes a look at examples of fish decoys made and used over the past 100 years, it becomes apparent that many of them don't resemble actual living species but, instead, are highly stylized in both color and design. At the same time, not all of them are simple and primitively made, for there is also a tradition of realistic fish decoy carving that challenges the expert woodcarver as well as the novice. In fact, many carvers go out of their way to copy every detail of a particular species, hoping that the more accurate a decoy is, the better it will attract the fish they want to catch. And today, the extreme refinement that contemporary bird and duck decoy carvers are putting into their work has influenced many fish decoy carvers, who are producing more realistic decoys than ever before.

This book therefore presents the basic design and techniques of traditional fish decoy carving as well as more advanced forms of the craft. The beginning woodcarver will find all the information about tools, materials, and carving techniques necessary for carving simple fish decoys. The experienced woodcarver who already has the tools and carving skills can apply them to this specialized craft and create some wonderfully unique and sophisticated decoys.

For the experienced fish decoy carver and spear fisherman, this book offers a chance to compare notes with a fellow craftsman and fisherman, with the acknowledgment that there are probably as many techniques and styles as there are carvers.

Finally, for the collector, this book presents an overview of the creative process, use, and history of fish decoys, which will enhance the knowledge and appreciation of one of the more obscure crafts in the American heritage at a time when serious collecting is just beginning.

1

Growing Up on the Ice

Ice fishing has long been the neglected child of American outdoor literature, while fly fishing (angling for trout, more precisely) has been the favored son. A number of American writers have had a fascination with fishing, if not a genuine love for the sport, and have acted on their motivation to write about it.

Ernest Hemingway put the Upper Peninsula and the little town of Seney on the map with his tale of trout fishing in "Big Two-Hearted River." Michigan's own Robert Traver has also extolled the merits and pleasures of trout fishing in his native state.

In these stories, though, as well as in the countless volumes of fishing literature that line the library shelves, scarcely a thing has been written about ice fishing. Admittedly, a Garrison Keillor monologue from "A Prairie Home Companion" takes us inside a shanty with some old men who talk more than they fish, chew snoose, spit when they want to, and tell racy jokes they wouldn't dare tell in the presence of their wives. But this isn't the kind of ice fishing I am talking about. These men were fishing for walleye with baited hooks that did not need much tending until a fish came looking for an easy meal. The ice fishing I am referring to, and the kind I was weaned on in Michigan's eastern Upper Peninsula, is spearing for pike.

The sport of ice fishing may not evoke the romantic picture of fish rising on a river or lake in the fresh morning air, as summertime angling often does, but it is hard to match the beauty of a huge golden moon on the rise above the eastern horizon, the western skyline still aglow from the setting sun, as you head for home after a day in the shanty. With the snow pure and white around you and the crisp freshness of the subzero temperatures adding snap to your footsteps, turning your breath into little clouds as you exhale, it feels good to be alive and enjoying winter's magic.

The only picture most people have of the sport, however, is that of the fisherman sitting alone in a dark shanty from sunup till sundown staring bleary-eyed into six feet of water, endlessly working his decoy up and down for a chance at a mere pike that may or may not be bold enough to present a decent target. To some, this sounds more like a direct route to cabin fever than a sport for pleasure and relaxation.

Now consider all the hard work of building your shanty in the bitter cold, hauling it miles over icy roads, dragging it across the lake where you labor in the freezing slush to cut through twelve to twenty inches of ice, then struggle with a pair of tongs hefting huge chunks of ice out of the water so that you can finally shove your shanty over the hole, block it, and bank it all around with snow. Furthermore, each day of fishing begins by chopping through three or four inches of new ice again. And don't forget to get your shanty out of there before spring breakup—it's the law.

Negatives? Well, you could see it that way. But in all my years of growing up in Sault Ste. Marie and fishing every winter from ice in till ice out, I never thought of them as such. In fact, the happiest and most cherished memories of my youth are the many hours and days I spent spearing for pike.

These fish may not be the most popular among fishermen, but there are those who see beauty in the pike's sleek and powerful body, his long, duck-billed face and menacing glare. To see him beneath the ice in six feet of crystal-clear water with his gold-green, camouflaged flanks glistening while his fins pump the water like a bull pawing the ground before an attack—this is a sight not quickly forgotten.

This old decoy was given to me by my brother. Next to it are a pike spear, an ice spud, and a well-used knapsack that doubles as a tackle bag and creel.

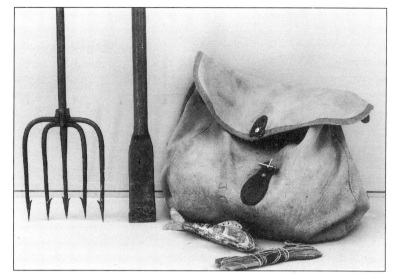

As far as edibility goes, when properly seasoned, stuffed, and baked or broiled to perfection, the pike is a more than satisfactory meal. And when soaked overnight in a good brine and slowly cured in a smokehouse, the large chunks of tender flesh that fall from the bones are a mouth-watering treat that is hard to refuse.

I believe much of the appeal of spearfishing lies in its simplicity. A spearman's equipment consists of two or three good decoys (preferably hand-made), a spear (usually of the ancient type), a hefty ice spud, a homemade shanty with a small stove inside, and warm clothing. There is no need to impress anyone with your gear, because there is seldom anybody interested enough in what you are doing to question it, just as there is usually no one except yourself to impress with your catches.

One of the best decoys I ever owned was handed down to me from my brother. It is still in my possession and looks about the same today as it did when he gave it to me. Most of the paint is worn off, the tail is loose, and the shape is extremely simple with no detailed carving at all. The fins and tail are of galvanized sheet metal, bent out of shape from years of use, but its swimming action is perfect: slow, smooth, and easily controlled by a slight tug on the jigging line. It has fooled many a pike into thinking it's a tasty meal.

5

This was the case one mild January day many years ago at Lake George on the east side of Sugar Island. I had gotten off to a late start that morning, and it was nearly eleven o'clock before I had cleared the hole, fired up the stove, and settled in to fish. The unusual pinkish glare of the thinly clouded sky and the stillness of the air that day sit in my memory as if it were just yesterday. The hue that flooded the sky also penetrated the ice and painted the sandy bottom the same color as the clouds.

My decoy had not been down for more than two minutes when there was a swirl of black and white in the center of the hole as a pike came in and hit the wooden fish at full speed. He took it with him under the shanty where the line held him, with only his tail and dorsal fin visible from above. I grabbed my spear and lowered it a few inches into the water, ready to let fly. I held the decoy line taut. As the pike began to drift into full view, I realized that it was just an overzealous "hammer handle" about eighteen inches long. I eased my spear out of the water and sat there waiting to see what the little menace was going to do next. He was still holding the

I speared this seven-pound northern pike on Munuscong Bay near Sault Ste. Marie. (Photo by Angus Phillips)

decoy in his toothy grasp when I decided to give a slight but quick tug on the line. That was all it took to spook him, and he disappeared in a flash.

This encounter was an omen of things to come that day. By five o'clock in the evening I had seen more than twenty pike, most of them in the eighteen- to twenty-inch range like the first one. On two occasions, a pair of small ones appeared in the hole and just stared at my decoy. When they had stared enough, they slowly swam away. In all my years of fishing, that was the only day I have seen two pike in the hole at the same time. Of all the fish that I saw, I speared only three, each in the four- or five-pound class. This is the way it is with spearing, though: You take what you are willing to clean and eat. The satisfaction of luring them in is often reward enough for your patience and effort.

That day was unusual. On a typical outing, coaxing in just three or four pike and spearing two of them were all I ever really expected.

There were slower times, too. I remember one especially cold, dark January day when, a teenager, I sat for hours pulling my decoy through all kinds of contortions without seeing a single fish. I tried every decoy in my bag, sometimes two at a time. I was getting no results, so I began to experiment. I adjusted the metal tail of my favorite decoy time and again so that it swam in broad circles, tight circles, medium circles. I made it swim slow, fast, just off the bottom, just under the ice. I tried everything and interested not a single fish. So I turned to various gimmicks I thought might be the key to the pike's mysterious behavior.

I rubbed the oil from canned sardines (which I had had for lunch) on my decoy to appeal to the fish's sense of smell. I wrapped the decoy in the tinfoil from my sandwich. I hung shiny doodads from it. I also hung a Dardevle down in the hole, believing that the sparkle emanating from it as it darted up and fluttered back down would attract pike a mile away. More ingeniously (I believed at the time), I hung buttons, forks, spoons, and even a red and white bandana in the water, all of which attracted nothing. I also had a tremendous (but controllable) urge to stick my head below the ice like a human periscope and peer beyond the narrow limits of the hole, so convinced was I that a gang of pike was lying just out of sight, attracted by the strange goings-on in the water but wise enough not to get too close.

When all of this had been done, and I had tried everything imaginable, I went back to a single, smooth-floating decoy. Within twenty minutes a sleek four-pounder came cruising in as if to make the point that tradition pays off. He also made it clear that the rules of the game are set by the fish, and if they are not willing to participate, there is little you can do to get them to join in.

Ice fishing is also not without its dangers, but most mishaps involve only disappointment, inconvenience, and loss of equipment. I recall one winter that was cut short by an unexpected warm spell in late February. Typically, you could wait out a thaw at this time of year and still get in a few more weeks of spearing once the weather turned cold again before the final breakup. But the cold did not return that year, and by the time I finally decided the thaw was going to hold, I set out one morning at daybreak with my friend and fishing companion, Jim McKiddie, to haul my shanty ashore. With spud in hand to probe the failing ice, we made our way toward my shanty. About halfway there, nearly a mile from shore, I dropped my spud to the ice as I had been doing with each step, and it plunged through, halfway up the handle.

"Did you see that?" I whispered to Jim, afraid that even a sound as loud as my voice would break the ice beneath my feet; if the crust was that thin two feet in front of us, what was the rest of it like?

The term *pussyfooting* has never meant as much to me as it did then, because that is exactly what we did, but not in the direction of my shanty. Instead, we made for shore, nearly kissed the ground when we got there, and stood contemplating the consequences of not having acted a few days sooner: My shanty was a goner along with a decent spear, a spud, a shovel, and four or five decoys. To make matters worse, if the shanty were to be found floating somewhere with my name and address on the door before it broke up or sank to the bottom, I would also be fined.

Of all the dangers of ice fishing, both real and imagined, the obvious possibility of falling through the large hole in the floor of the spearman's shanty and drowning in the frigid waters beneath the ice is the most dreaded.

It was many years ago when my Uncle Russell and Aunt Rita decided to try their luck on Raber Bay. They had been fishing the better part of the morning in separate shanties not far from each other when Uncle Russell heard his wife calling for him. Think-

For many who grow up in the North Country, it's enjoyable to spend a cold and stormy winter's day in the fish shanty. Note the runners fastened to the side. (Photo by James Cottle)

ing Aunt Rita had speared a big fish and needed help getting it up, my uncle untied his spear and — with no great urgency — made his way over to her shanty. When he opened the door, he couldn't believe his eyes. For there was Rita lying face down on the floor stretched across the one-and-a-half by five-foot hole; icy water lapped the edge of the hole just inches from her face as she clung precariously to a bit of floor frame on the far side of the shanty.

Aunt Rita got herself into this predicament when she tried to spear a fish, slipped, and fell forward. She saved herself from taking the plunge by grabbing the frame, but in that position she couldn't find enough leverage to get back up.

Uncle Russell took a firm hold of her jacket but made no move to lift her. "Rita," he said, "did you get the fish?"

But these, too, are the ways of ice fishing. Hardships, dangers, and occasional mishaps are part of the sport. And along with them come many lessons for life: patience, concentration, hard work, self-reliance, and a respect and appreciation for nature.

One old fellow I often fished with went so far as to base many of his opinions about people on what he had learned from ice fishing. "You can tell a lot about a man by the way he fishes," he once said. "It's a lazy man who lets his decoy dangle lifeless at the end of the string half the time. You've got to keep it moving— that's what the fish like. A man who spears more than he can eat is lacking in respect for mankind, too. Show me a man who thinks he's got to catch fish every time he goes out, and I'll show you a man who thinks the world owes him a living."

I was young when the old man spun his philosophy about ice fishing and life, and it seemed to make enough sense to me that I did not question it. And I have never felt the need to put it to the test since then. For the myths of youth in a world of computerized data and scientific facts are like breaths of fresh air in the dog days of August. And for all I know, there just might be more to the sport of ice fishing than meets the eye.

2

Ice Fishing and Fish Decoys

Fish decoys, in their present form and use, probably originated among the Native Americans of Alaska, Canada, and the Great Lakes region. The oldest examples in existence today were fashioned from stones, bones, antlers, and shells. We can assume that some of the earliest fish decoys were also carved from wood but did not withstand the test of time, as did those made from harder materials.

The early decoys were crude representations of small fish, often weighted with stones or other heavy objects to make them sink in the water beneath the ice of a frozen river or lake. A fisherman would lie in wait on the ice above with his head covered by skins or blankets that diminished the light, allowing him to see deep into the clear water below. In one hand he held a line connected to his decoy, which he jigged up and down with a swimming motion in an attempt to attract a larger fish to prey upon the replica. In his other hand the fisherman held a crude, harpoonlike spear. When he was successful in attracting a fish to his decoy, he coaxed it into spearing range. He then thrust his spear into the unsuspecting fish, pulled it up through the hole, and laid it out on the ice to freeze.

This was one of the methods the Native Americans used to supply themselves with food during the harsh cold winter months in the North.

This kind of winter spearfishing has gone on for hundreds of years, judging from the prehistoric artifacts that have been found near the Great Lakes. Early written verification dates back to the 1700s, when European explorers observed these methods and learned them from the Indians.

For a more thorough discussion of the history of spearfishing and the identification of old fish decoys, I recommend the books by Art, Brad, and Scott Kimball listed in the bibliography. The Kimballs are researchers and collectors whose work on the subject is unsurpassed.

CONTEMPORARY METHODS

The winter spearfishing developed by our Native Americans and the fish decoy itself have changed very little over the centuries. In fact, many American Indians intent on preserving their cultural heritage and the customs of their ancestors spear for pike and muskies today using the same techniques as their forefathers. This is particularly true of the Ojibway Indians of the Lac du Flambeau region of Wisconsin.

Winter spearfishing with the use of a decoy has long been a method of sport fishing among American Indians and non-Indians alike. It was practiced in most of the midwestern states, New York, and New England well into this century, and it still thrives today—with some restrictions—in Michigan, Minnesota, and Wisconsin.

With few exceptions, fish decoys are made to attract pike, muskies, and sturgeons. There is usually no difference between the decoys made for pike and those made for muskies, because these fish often share the same habitat and prey on common victims. Sturgeon decoys, however, are much larger than pike and musky decoys. They're intended to attract these huge fish strictly out of the fish's curiosity or desire to congregate with other fish. Sturgeon don't attack the decoy with the intention of eating it, as the pike and muskies do. Considering these primary differences, in

A model of a fish shanty.
Most pike fishermen pre-
fer to sit on a stool or
bench while they fish. A
small wood stove com-
monly provides heat, hot
coffee, and even a warm
meal.

this book I have chosen to deal only with decoys made and used for pike and musky fishing.

Building the shanty. Although the winter spear fisherman has taken advantage of some modern conveniences to add a few creature comforts to the sport, little has changed since the European settlers began spearfishing from a shanty.

The fish shanty (also called a shack, dark house, icehouse, or spearing house) usually ranges in size from four feet (1.2 m) square to six feet (1.8 m) square and is tall enough so that the spearman can stand up inside. It's commonly constructed of cardboard over a one-inch (2.5 cm) by two-inch (5.1 cm) wooden stud frame covered on the outside with waterproof tar paper. Some fishermen, however, cover the frame with quarter-inch (.64 cm) plywood instead of cardboard; these structures last longer but are much more cumbersome to haul around.

It's very important that the shanty block out all external light so that the fisherman can see deep into the water below. This darkness inside also lessens the chance that a fish will catch the movements of the fisherman and disappear before it can be speared.

No matter what the wall covering is made of, its frame is nailed to a floor made of plywood or three-quarter-inch (1.9 cm) planking over a two-by-four (5.1 cm by 10.2 cm) frame. A small wood, oil, or (more recently) propane stove keeps the fisherman warm and the spear and hole free of ice.

The hole in the floor of the shanty gives the fisherman a good view of the lake bottom. It's typically fifteen (38.1 cm) to eighteen inches (46 cm) wide and extends all the way across one side of the shanty. Some fishermen, however, prefer the hole in the center of the floor with seats situated in three corners and a stove in the fourth.

The avid fisherman sets out his shanty at the start of the spearing season or as soon as he feels the ice is safe, usually when it's at least four (10.2 cm) or five inches (12.7 cm) thick. And later in the winter, when the ice has become much thicker, he may want to move his shanty to a different location on the lake. For this reason, many spearmen build their shanties with runners permanently attached to one side, so that when they make a move it's simply a matter of tipping the shanty onto the runners and sliding it across the ice.

Setting up to fish. As the winter season advances, the ice cover on a lake or river will often reach thicknesses of two feet (61 cm) or more. This means that cutting and clearing a hole five feet (1.5 m) long and eighteen inches (46 cm) wide is no simple matter. It is therefore important that the ice fisherman have the proper tools for the job.

The main tool used for cutting the hole is a long-handled heavy iron chisel known as an ice spud. The fisherman prepares to cut the hole by first clearing the snow from the spot he has chosen for his shanty. He then marks off a hole just a little larger than the one in the floor of the shanty. If the ice isn't too thick, the job can be completed with the ice spud alone. But when it's a foot or more thick, cutting it with the spud becomes a long, hard job.

Most spear fishermen who have been at the sport for many years own a good ice saw, which is usually five or six feet (1.5 or 1.8 m) long, has a handle at one end, and two-inch (5.1 cm) teeth all running in the same direction. Today, some fishermen have broken with tradition and use a chain saw instead.

Before using the ice saw, a slot must be cut with the ice spud to get the saw blade started. The fisherman tries to cut the hole so that the edges are angled out at the bottom to give him a little more vision into the periphery under the shanty.

Once all four sides of the hole are sawed, the fisherman is left with one large, solid block of ice that must be lifted out of the water. This is best done by breaking it up into three or four smaller pieces and pulling them out with a good pair of ice tongs. The shanty is then moved over the hole.

When in place, each corner of the shanty must be raised slightly and supported by two-by-fours a couple of inches (5.1 cm) off the ice so that the floor frame will not become stuck when the

Spear fishermen in Michigan's Eastern Upper Peninsula are a solitary lot. They'll usually select a spot for their shanty far away from the next fellow. Here, Ron Edgerly (an avid spearman from Sault Ste. Marie) looks on as I start a hole with a power auger. The snowmobile tracks represent one of the few modern additions (along with power augers, chainsaws, and propane stoves) that have come to the sport of spearfishing in over 100 years. (Photo by Angus Phillips)

water around the freshly cut hole freezes. This must be done periodically throughout the winter so that the floor remains clear of the continual buildup of surface ice. Many a fisherman has had to burn his shanty down because he didn't attend to it regularly and the floor became buried in a foot (30.5 cm) or more of ice.

The spear on the left was produced commercially and purchased in a sporting goods store. The one on the right is an old, hand-forged model. Both are true pike spears. The one in the center is a hand-made herring spear with the shank and tines set in lead; many pike fishermen prefer this style over the other two.

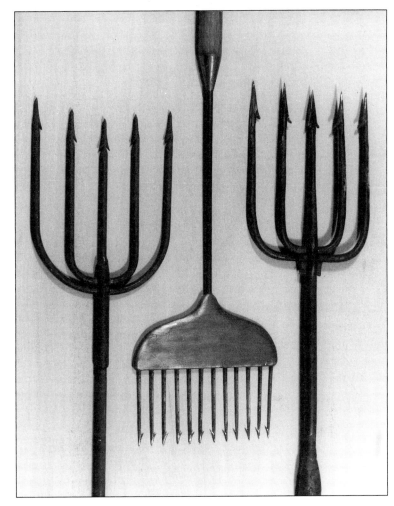

Once the shanty is in place and blocked properly, all four sides must be banked with snow so that no light from outside will cause reflections on the water and interfere with the visibility of movement underwater.

Finally, before settling in to fish, the fisherman must clear the hole of the small ice chips and slush that remain in the water. Most fishermen find a screen strainer or sieve, such as one used for draining vegetables or noodles in the kitchen, to be perfect for the job. This must be done not only on the day when the spearman first sets out his shanty, but on each subsequent day of fishing as well.

Fishing. Most pike and musky fishermen prefer to sit on a chair, bench, or stool while spending a whole day in their shanty. Others build a low rail, about fifteen inches (38.1 cm) high, in front of the hole and kneel on sacks of straw instead of sitting. Many spearmen in the Sault Ste. Marie, Michigan, area do this, which is probably a carry-over from the old-time herring spearing that was once popular in the region.

But no matter whether the fisherman kneels or sits in his shanty, there are two essential items he uses to attract and subdue his game: a decoy and a spear.

The pike spear usually has five or seven tines six to ten inches (15.2 to 25.4 cm) long, about the thickness of a pencil. Each tine has a barb an inch (2.5 cm) or so from the tip so that once a fish is speared, it can't easily slip away. Many pike spears are hand-forged, crude, vicious-looking affairs with a four- or five-foot (1.2 or 1.5 m) wooden or metal handle attached to a shank welded to the tines. More refined spears have been manufactured by various companies over the years, and some are still available at sporting goods stores in the North.

A popular spear used for pike in the Sault Ste. Marie area is one that was developed for herring rather than pike. These spears are made by setting eleven or thirteen tines about one-eighth inch (.32 cm) in diameter and five inches (12.7 cm) long into a carved wooden mold three quarters of an inch (1.9 cm) apart. A shank for the handle is laid in the top and the mold is filled with melted lead. Once the lead is hard and cool, the wooden form is pulled away, the lead is shaped and balanced with a rasp, and a handle — usually of wood — is attached.

Many pike fishermen swear by these spears. They believe that if the tines are close enough together, there is a good chance one will find the spine and paralyze the fish, thus avoiding a struggle and a chance of losing the catch.

Most fishermen tie their spears to the wall of the shanty with a length of rope fastened to the end of the handle. The rope is long enough to allow the spear to reach at least to the same depth as the decoy, which may be no more than two or three feet (61 or 91 cm) below the ice or as far down as fifteen feet (4.6 m). Spearing becomes difficult beyond ten or twelve feet (3.1 or 3.7 m).

The purpose of the pike and musky decoy is to fool these predatory fish into attacking what they think is a typical food-fish or other delectable critter that they've devoured many times before. Therefore, the majority of fishermen prefer a decoy that represents a small version of a fish that exists in the local waters. But other creatures that these voracious feeders are thought to prey upon, such as frogs, mice, ducklings, muskrats, and even turtles, are also made into decoys.

Probably the two most important elements the spear fisherman looks for in a good fish decoy are the body shape and the swimming action. Most decoys that represent fish are carved in a shape that is easily identified as that of a particular species, and nearly every freshwater species has been carved over the years.

When it comes to painting the decoy, however, the fisherman is not always concerned with accurate, representational colors. In this matter, he sees the decoy more as an attention-getter and attractor than a true imitation of a living creature. You'll find fish decoys painted in just about every color combination and pattern imaginable.

The swimming action of a fish decoy is also very important to the ice fisherman, but not everyone agrees upon what is best. Some spearmen like a heavy decoy that swims in fast, tight circles; others like a slow, smooth-floating decoy that they can more easily control with the line and jigging stick.

The jigging stick is a piece of wood cut and shaped to hold a few yards of heavy fishing line strong enough to withstand the attack of a large fish. The decoy is fastened to the line with a snap swivel that allows for easy change of decoys and prevents the line from becoming twisted.

Some fishermen will hold this stick in one hand all day, constantly varying the depth of the decoy by winding and unwinding line on the stick. Others simply use the jigging stick to store the decoy line and, instead of holding the stick, hang it on the ceiling or wall above the hole once they have let out enough line to get the decoy to the desired depth in the water. They then work the decoy by pulling on the line itself. (Three kinds of jigging sticks are pictured in Chapter 10.)

In any case, the fisherman pulls his decoy up and down, watching it swim with a circular motion determined by the slight curve in the tail. If the tail is made of metal or some other flexible material, the size of the circle can be adjusted occasionally by bending the tail this way or that.

Once a pike or musky decides to investigate this commotion under the ice, the spearman must be ready for anything. These big fish are apt to attack a decoy so fast and furiously that they can snap heavy fishing line like a piece of thread. Or they may approach ever so slowly and cautiously, staying just out of spearing range until the fisherman entices them in with just the right moves of his decoy. The slightest false twitch of the line or turn of the decoy can cause a wary fish to vanish in an instant and never return.

When a fish does make the mistake of swimming into spearing range and pauses long enough for the fisherman to have a chance at it, a good spearman usually won't miss. The fish is speared, hauled out of the water, and laid out on the ice where Mother Nature's refrigerator keeps it fresh for the oven or frying pan.

FISH DECOYS FOR THE CARVER

For the carver of fish decoys, I believe it is important to understand the sport of ice fishing and the role fish decoys play in this sport. They originated as functional objects and retain that function today. A decoy that doesn't work properly in the water might be nice to look at, but in reality it is no good as a decoy.

For me, much of the charm of a fish decoy is its potential to fool a big pike or musky into thinking it has an easy victim waiting to be eaten. This is what makes fish-decoy carving a craft unto itself, different from fish carving.

While taking advantage of some of the modern tools and materials available to us today, we can still work within the tradition of fish-decoy carving as it has been practiced for over two hundred years. This is because even with these new tools and materials, function is basic; extremely realistic detail carved and painted on the body of a fish decoy is essentially decoration aimed more at humans than at fish.

FISH DECOYS FOR THE COLLECTOR

Understanding the sport of ice fishing and the craft of fish-decoy making provides insight for the collector at a time when old fish decoys are being sold and auctioned for thousands of dollars. Unfortunately, along with these exorbitant prices come unscrupulous dealers out to make fast money at someone else's expense. Deliberate fakes have already shown up and are being passed off as authentic. The collector must be aware of this and, at the very least, examine each decoy carefully for proper wear and carver-identification marks. It's not asking too much to see the decoy work in the water either, or to require written proof of authenticity.

There are still many fish-decoy carvers working today who understand both the craft and sport of ice fishing. Buying directly from them is one way of getting a contemporary decoy at a fair and honest price. Consult the Kimball books as your guide for collecting fish decoys both old and new.

3

Basic Woodcarving

This chapter is primarily meant for the novice carver who needs some basic tips on work space, tools, materials, and simple carving techniques. The more advanced carver may also want to glance through it for advice pertaining directly to the craft of fish-decoy carving.

WORK SPACE

Before beginning your first project, find yourself a work space that is well lit and has both a solid table to work on and a comfortable chair to sit in. You're going to produce many wood chips and raise a lot of dust, so consider ease of cleanup too. You'll also need to have access to a hot plate or gas burner for melting lead if you don't have a lead-melting pot. And be sure the room where you melt the lead is well ventilated so that the toxic fumes from the melting lead can escape.

BASIC EQUIPMENT

If you have never carved before and are reluctant to use a sharp knife close to your fingers, you may want to carve the body of your

Your work area doesn't have to be large. I do most of my carving on my lap and the rest of the work on a sturdy table. My work space may look cluttered, but everything I need is within easy reach.

decoy with a wood rasp and sandpaper rather than a knife—you can add details with a woodburning pen. A wood rasp is also a good tool for children to start with. You'll be surprised by some of the results they can achieve on a piece of soft pine or basswood.

But for the adult who is new to woodcarving, the best way to eliminate the fear of cutting yourself with the knife and to gain confidence in your carving ability is to keep the blade as sharp as possible and protect yourself properly. Wear a good, hefty apron (preferably leather), a tight-fitting batter's glove on your holding hand, and a leather thumb guard (tape or an adhesive bandage such as a Band-Aid will suffice) on your carving hand.

The best all-purpose knife for the beginning carver is a German-style chip-carving knife. It has a nicely contoured handle about five inches long with a short, jackknife-style blade. I provide this knife for the students in my classes and find that both the novice and the experienced carvers like it for everything from roughing out their decoys to carving detail.

BASIC TECHNIQUES

Once you have your decoy blank, which consists of the basic pattern of your decoy cut out of wood and ready to carve, draw a centerline the length of the back and underside. This will help to orient you on the center while you carve, which makes it easier to keep your decoy symmetrical. You may also want to draw on all sides lines that depict the shape you'd like your finished carving to have. Don't be afraid to draw anything on your blank that you think will help.

For carving a fish decoy, there are basically five carving strokes you'll need to use. The best stroke, and the one you'll feel the most comfortable with, is the pull stroke, also called the paring stroke. This can be done in two ways. Grasp the blank with your holding hand at the end farther from your body and brace the thumb of your carving hand against the end of the blank that is next to you. Now, simply push with your thumb and pull the knife toward you by closing the hand; let the muscles of your fingers and wrist do the work. To avoid cutting your thumb, keep it out of the way just under the blank below the point where the knife will come off the end. But if you wear a thumb guard, you won't have to worry if your thumb happens to get in the way.

There is a variation on this pull stroke which will allow you to make longer, smoother cuts. Hold your blank at the end farther from your body, brace the other end against your apron (this is

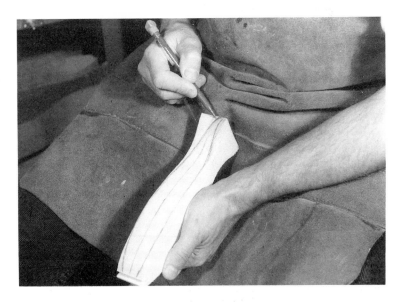

Draw a centerline on the back and belly of your blank. This will help you to maintain symmetry while you carve. Draw any additional lines that may help.

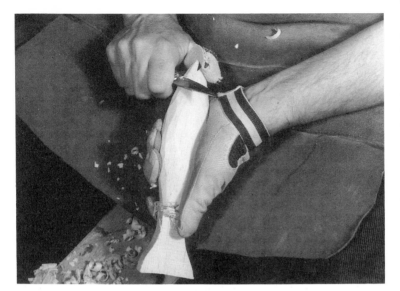

The pull (or paring) stroke is essential to all kinds of carving. Brace your thumb against the end of the blank and pull the knife toward you by closing the hand. A thumb guard protects your thumb should you happen to bump the knife blade against it. A leather glove and apron give additional protection.

where leather is nice) and hold your elbows tight to your sides, allowing your hands only a few inches of movement. Now pull your knife toward you just shaving the surface. This will allow you to take long, smooth strokes that give your decoy a nicely textured surface, which you might prefer to leave, as I do, rather than sand it smooth. (See the photo in Chapter 6.)

You'll also need to learn the push stroke, of which there are two variations. The standard stroke is the one used by anyone who has ever whittled a point on a stick for roasting marshmallows. Hold your blank at the end closer to your body and whittle away at the opposite end. This is a fast method of removing wood with a knife, but you don't have much control with it. Be careful not to take off too much wood, and keep your knees well clear of the blade as it comes off the end of your blank.

There is a variation of the push stroke that is especially useful when control, rather than wood removal, is the goal. Hold your blank at a point behind the area you want to carve. With the knife blade facing away from you, use the thumb of the holding hand to push the blade forward. At the same time, pull the knife handle toward you so that your thumb acts as a fulcrum, creating a lever action. Although this restricts you to making cuts only as long as your thumb will reach, you'll have excellent control of the blade for fine detailing you might not be able to do otherwise.

The last carving technique that you'll want to master is the basic method used in chip carving. It actually relies on both the push and the pull strokes explained above and is essential for carving fine details on your decoy. Rather than explaining it here, however, I'll leave it for the section in Chapter 6 on detailing your decoy. At that point you'll already have developed a feel for your tools and wood and will be ready for more intricate carving.

THE WOOD

This brings us to an important consideration that not only beginning but also experienced carvers must take into account: the character of the wood itself.

No matter what kind of wood you're using, you must be aware of the contour of the grain at all times. It isn't always obvious on the surface, so you must develop a feel for it as you carve. If you have never carved before, practice on a scrap piece of wood, the same kind from which you'll carve your decoy. This will give you the chance to practice the various carving strokes.

The way to feel out the grain is to begin carving close to that end of your blank toward which you are cutting. Move farther

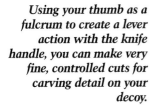

Using your thumb as a fulcrum to create a lever action with the knife handle, you can make very fine, controlled cuts for carving detail on your decoy.

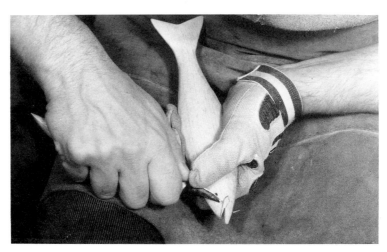

away from that end until you come to a point where your knife catches the grain and threatens to pull out a larger piece than you bargained for because it has started splitting the wood. You must then attack this point from the other direction. Either change your stroke and carve in the opposite direction, or turn your piece of wood around. It will not be long before you have the feel of the wood and understand just what the grain is doing.

SHARPENING

Any good craftsman must see to it that his tools are kept as sharp as possible. Carving with a dull knife leads to shoddy workmanship and can be dangerous for the carver. A dull knife can often skip over the wood surface and accidentally catch the fingers or hand. The extra exertion applied to compensate for a dull blade can also lead to injury. So a little time taken now and then to keep your knife razor-sharp is time well spent.

Initially, you'll want to hone your knife on a whetstone. There are many stones available either at the hardware store or from a carving-tool supplier. But you'll really only need to buy one for all your common sharpening. I recommend a stone with a different grit on each side. One side should be coarse or medium for heavy-duty honing and the other side smooth for finishing. You'll sel-

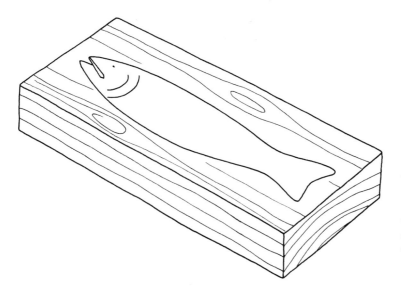

The grain of the wood should always run lengthwise on your blank. The thickness of the blank should be just slightly greater than your finished decoy.

Sharpen your knife by moving it in a circular motion on a whetstone covered with a few drops of oil. Sharpen one side of the blade, then the other. Keep the cutting edge flat and the back edge at a twenty- to thirty-degree angle to the stone.

dom need the coarse side, except when you have a nick in your blade or have broken it and need to reshape it.

To get a good edge on a new knife (most don't come fully sharpened), use the smooth side of your stone. Spread a little honing oil (all-purpose household oil will do) on the stone, lay your knife on it with the cutting edge flat and the back of the blade at a 20- to 30-degree angle. Move it in a circular motion. Turn it over, and do the same to the other side.

To get the perfect edge on your knife, refine it by polishing it on a leather strop after you've sharpened it on the stone. You can easily make yourself a strop by cutting a strip of leather from an old belt, purse, or jacket. It should be about ten inches (25.4 cm) long and two or three inches (5.1 or 7.6 cm) wide. Place your knife on it as you did on the whetstone. This time, instead of moving it in a circular motion, stroke away from the cutting edge, first on one side, then on the other. Repeat this for twenty or thirty strokes. Now, test it on a scrap piece of wood for sharpness. A sharp knife will leave a smooth cut with no sign of tearing or crunching the wood.

A leather power-strop will reduce your sharpening time to a minimum. I keep my wheel in a reversible drill mounted on my workbench. Always make sure the wheel is turning away from the cutting edge before you lay your knife on it.

If you strop your knife often enough—whenever you feel it's losing its best edge—you'll scarcely need to use the whetstone. And if you invest a few dollars in a power strop (a leather wheel mounted on a shaft to fit your electric drill), the whole process of sharpening can be reduced to a minimum and you can spend more time carving.

4

Tools and Materials

Traditionally, fish decoy carvers, being a practical bunch, didn't spend much time searching the lumberyards for that perfect piece of wood from which to carve their subject. More often than not, they searched the scrap pile in their own backyards and ended up carving their favorite decoys from discarded two-by-fours (5.1 cm by 10.2 cm) as well as from pieces of expensive hardwoods. As a rule, a good pocketknife was all they needed to complete the job. They also painted their decoys with just about any colors available around the house from natural stains and dyes to super-gloss fingernail polish or artists' oils. The custom among American Indian carvers was to shade their decoys simply by burning the wood darker where desired.

Lead, nuts and bolts, stones, and other heavy small objects sufficed to weight their decoys. They usually placed these items inside the hollowed-out belly, but sometimes they simply tied them onto the underside with thread, fishing line, or a leather thong.

As for the hardware, you'll find old fish decoys sporting fins and tails fashioned from coffee cans, tobacco cans, copper, brass, and leather. Tacks and nails commonly represent eyes, although many a carver has plundered his tackle box and taken the glass eyes off old fishing plugs to use on his decoys. Even the eyes from a discarded doll or teddy bear can add the final touch that brings a fish decoy to life.

As you see, you don't have to invest a fortune to carve a good, functional fish decoy. But by using a few good tools and materials, you'll be able to master the craft more quickly and with more satisfying results.

Therefore, this chapter presents not only the basic tools and materials essential to fish-decoy carving, but also modern-day equipment and supplies that will help make your job of carving and metalworking a little easier and your decoys better.

Supplies needed for painting your decoy are included in the chapter on painting. A list of tool and supply sources can be found in the appendix; any items you can't get locally can be ordered through one or more of these.

TOOLS

Sawing. Before actually carving your decoy, you need to cut its basic shape from the wood you've decided to use. For this task, a simple *coping saw* is all you'll really need. But if you have a *band saw*, or even a *scroll saw*, it will make your job a bit easier.

Carving. Carving knives come in many shapes, sizes, and price ranges. But if you have a good *jackknife*, preferably with a locking blade, you're already in business and don't really need to buy another. My favorite knife, however, is a simple German-style chip-carving knife. It has a long, comfortable handle and a short, narrow blade. It's an inexpensive knife and is excellent for carving the body of your decoy as well as adding detail.

Look over the many knives at your local woodcarving supply store, get a feel for the knife that's right for you, and stick with it until it no longer fits your needs. If you don't have a variety of knives to choose from locally, the catalog sources in the appendix will offer you just about everything that's available.

Beyond the carving knife, my favorite carving tool is the *drawknife*. It consists of a single blade with a wooden handle attached to each end and comes in a variety of lengths and widths with different handle contours as well. It's important to find the style best suited for you. The drawknife can be both pushed and pulled over your workpiece, and it will save you a good deal of time and effort in roughing out your decoy.

One other hand tool you might find useful, especially for texturing the body of your decoy, is a small *gouge.* You may also want to use it when you hollow out the belly of your decoy.

Many woodcarvers today do much of their carving with *power carvers.* These include machines with reciprocating chisel-style blades and the popular high-speed flexible shaft grinders. They can be purchased as attachments for your standard power drill or as complete units in themselves. Cutting wheels in an array of shapes, sizes, and cutting surfaces are available to handle just about any carving job you'll tackle. If you already own one of these machines, you've probably learned how to deal with the large

These are three typical knives used for carving fish decoys: a Swedish knife for rough-carving, a German chip-carving knife that is great for detail work, and a three-bladed jackknife that can be used for both rough-carving and detailing.

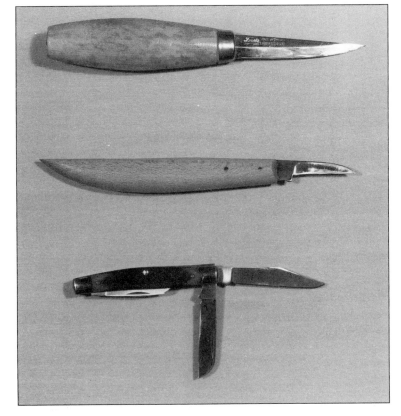

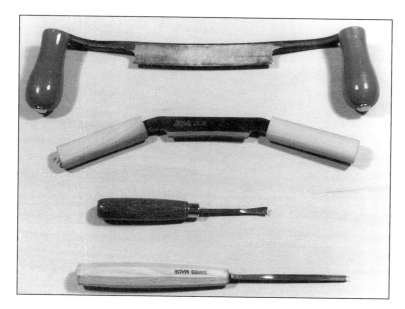

The two drawknives pictured here are good for quick wood removal. The gouges can be used for detailing the body and digging out the belly.

amounts of dust it raises and will want to use it, since it's a great time- and labor-saver. However, a power carver is not at all necessary for carving good fish decoys and, if you're any kind of traditionalist, you may feel that it detracts from the simplicity of the craft and sport.

Sanding. If you keep your knife as sharp as possible, you won't really have to do much sanding, provided you like the look of the carve marks on your finished decoy, as I do. However, if you want it to appear smooth and even, or if you want to texture the surface with a scale effect, you'll have to sand your decoy.

Sandpaper in medium and fine grades is all you'll really need. And for the hard-to-get-at places, use an *emery board*, made for manicuring fingernails. You can also make yourself some *sanding sticks* by glueing pieces of sandpaper to dowels of the diameters that fit your needs.

For extremely rough sanding, you'll find a *wood rasp* or *file* useful. In fact, as a youngster, I made my first fish decoys using only a rasp and sandpaper.

There are also many grinding and sanding attachments available for your electric drill and flexible shaft grinder to speed up and ease the task of sanding your decoy.

Hollowing. The belly of your decoy will have to be hollowed out and filled with lead to make the decoy sink in the water. This can be done with your carving knife or a small chisel, but an *electric drill* with a quarter-inch (.64 cm) bit will give you a more precise cut in half the time with half the effort. A *drill press* is even better. Some carvers use the *Forstner bit* for hollowing out decoys, but I prefer the *brad point bit*; the sharp point on the end prevents the bit from jumping from side to side as you begin each cut. This bit also clears the debris from the hole better than the Forstner bit.

You'll want to use your drill with a smaller bit when you mount the eyes, fins, and line-tie.

Woodburning. A *woodburning pen* is strictly optional, depending upon how much detail, if any, you want to add to your decoy. But a simple pen with two or three different tips is quite inexpensive and will probably suffice.

Expensive woodburning systems are available with a dozen different tips and temperature controls for the precise feathering you see on world-class bird and duck decoy carvings today.

Metalworking. If you decide to make the fins, tail, and eyes for your decoy out of metal, you'll need a pair of *tin snips* or *metal*

Fish decoys can be carved with a wood rasp like the one seen here along with various sanding sticks. Third from the top is a common emery board.

shears to cut them out. If you don't have a pair around the house, they're available at just about any hardware store. Get the pair that will cut the tightest turns. A pair of metal shears used by jewelers will do the best job. If you can't find them locally, you can easily order them. Sometimes a stout pair of household shears will cut metal too, but don't plan to use them for much else afterwards. An alternative to the metal shears is a *jeweler's saw* or coping saw with a fine, metal-cutting blade.

You'll need a pair of *pliers* and a pair of *wire cutters*. If you have a pair of pliers that are also wire cutters, they're perfect. Use a *hammer* and an *anvil* (a flat piece of hard steel) to flatten and texture your fins and tail after you've cut them out.

A *circle cutter* for the eyes is nice to have for making perfect circles, but it's rather expensive. There are other ways to cut cir-

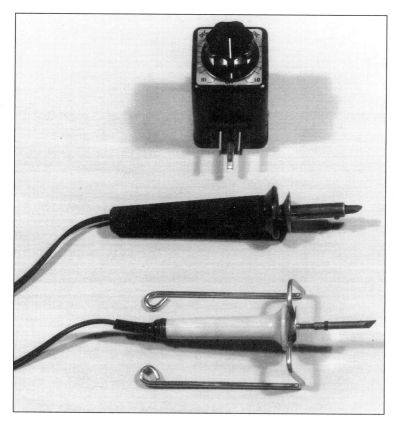

Woodburning pens are ideal for adding fins and tail rays to fish decoys. The heat regulator allows for precise detailing.

Two types of metal shears above the jeweler's saw, a pair of long-nose pliers, and a wire cutter. The grip on the second pair of shears (called plate shears) is easy on the hands and the blades are curved to allow for tight turns.

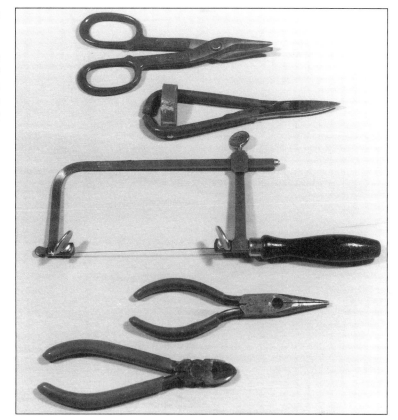

cles, and you can use many ready-made items for decoy eyes as well. If you want to make metal eyes yourself, then you'll need a *soldering iron* in order to attach a wire pin to the back of the eyes. Some woodburning tools will double as a soldering iron as well.

Finally, you'll find that a small *metal file* will come in handy if you want to refine the edges of the metal you've cut.

Leading. Melting lead for your decoy is not as big a problem as it may seem. In a pinch, you can melt it in a tin can on the kitchen stove, provided you have the proper ventilation to let the toxic fumes escape.

Better yet, find yourself an old *cast-iron frying pan* and a *hot plate.* Move outside or into the basement near an open window and do your leading there. You'll also want easy access to a *sink* or

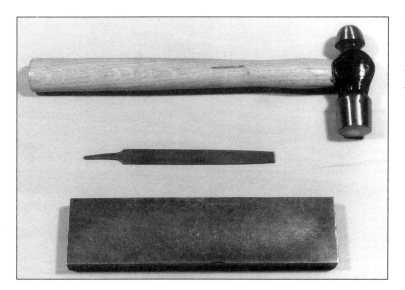

Use a hammer, metal file, and anvil (a piece of steel plating) to flatten, mottle, and refine the fins after cutting them.

tub (a large *ice chest* will do) filled with water to cool the lead and test your decoy as you weight it.

If you don't mind investing in an electric *lead-melting pot*, made exclusively for melting lead, there are at least two types available. They're very reliable and make this potentially dangerous task as safe and easy as possible.

Working safely. I can't put enough emphasis on the need for safety when carving fish decoys. There is potential for serious injury in just about every phase of the craft. If you're aware of this, stay alert at all times, and take the proper safety precautions, no injuries should occur.

To begin with, wear comfortable clothing that doesn't fit too loosely. I highly recommend a *leather apron.* It can protect you against minor mishaps and will provide a solid surface against which you can brace your decoy while carving it. I personally like to wear a tight-fitting leather *batter's glove* on my left hand to hold the piece of wood I'm carving. It not only protects the hand—at least somewhat—from the knife blade, but also provides a better grip on the blank. When leading, I wear a pair of *leather work gloves* in case I accidentally spill or pour molten lead on my hands.

Two types of lead-melting pots. The one on the left is easy and safe to use. A ladle or large spoon is recommended for dipping lead from the pot on the right.

Safety glasses are an absolute must, and you should get yourself a comfortable pair that you don't mind wearing the whole time you're working on your decoy.

It's a good idea to wear a *dust mask* whenever you're sawing or sanding, and a *chemical mask* while melting lead and painting your decoy. *Ear protectors* will guard against potential ear damage while you're hammering on the anvil.

MATERIALS

Wood. There are two important considerations in choosing your wood for fish decoys: availability and workability. Hardwoods are strong and durable, but carving decoys from them can be a slow and difficult process. I don't recommend them unless you're an experienced carver and know what you're up against. However, *poplar* and *aspen* are manageable hardwoods you may want to try. *Birch* and *maple*, being indigenous to the Great Lakes region, are two types of hardwood traditionally used for fish decoys.

I recommend the softer woods, such as basswood, sugar pine, white pine, and cedar. Most lumber companies carry these woods or can at least get them for you. If not, you can order them yourself from some of the suppliers listed in the appendix.

I personally prefer to use *sugar pine*, not only for carving fish decoys, but for most of my woodcarving projects. It's a clear pine, with few knots and a tight grain that's easy to manage but prominent enough to add character to a finished carving. It's available in a variety of thicknesses up to four inches (10.2 cm), but to carve the decoys presented in this book, you won't need anything thicker than one-and-one-half-inch (3.8 cm) stock.

Basswood is probably the most popular wood among carvers because it's very soft, has predictable grain patterns, and is usually easy to find in different lengths and widths. One problem I find with basswood, especially for fish decoys, is that unless it has been sealed thoroughly, it doesn't weather well when frequently exposed to the elements.

Cedar, although often knotty and coarse-grained (especially red cedar, which is the most common), weathers exceptionally well and is often used for fish decoys.

Clear white pine is probably the wood most easily obtained. This is fine for carving, provided it's good-quality white pine. The poorer grades will give you trouble with knots and unmanageable grain.

The bottom line when choosing the wood for your fish decoys is this: Nearly any type available will do, as long as you feel comfortable working with it.

Wood filler. You're going to need a good, waterproof wood filler, primarily to finish filling the belly cavity after you've added the lead. But wood filler is also a carver's best friend when unexpected chips and cracks need to be repaired.

I use white *Famowood Wood Plastic* most of the time, but *DAP Wood Dough* and *Plastic Wood* do an equally good job. If you use another type of wood filler, test it first to be sure that it's impervious to water before you apply it to your decoy.

Hardware: fins and tail, line-tie, and eyes. Fish decoys are generally made with *metal fins* and, often, a *metal tail* that can be adjusted while fishing. In choosing your metal, the primary factor to consider is its thickness and rigidity. You must be able to cut it with your shears or saw. Just about any metal will work. Tin cans, aluminum cans, stovepipes, signs, bicycle fenders, and scores of other items can all be cut and shaped into fins for fish decoys. But three commonly used metals are *galvanized sheet metal*, *brass*, and *copper*.

I prefer brass and copper for both their workability (provided they're not too heavy and rigid) and their appearance on the decoy. They can be treated with patina solutions, such as *liver of sulphur*, to control their appearance somewhat. The best source for these metals is the scrapyard, where they're usually sold by the pound. Jewelry suppliers also sell small sheets of brass and copper.

The fins and tail can be made from *wood* or *leather* as well, but leather tends to rot when it's exposed to water repeatedly, and wooden fins tend to break off (although wooden tails are very common on fish decoys). Both wood and leather add buoyancy to the decoy, which must be compensated for with additional lead in the belly.

The *line-tie* is usually nothing more than a small *screw eye*, placed just behind the head, to which the jigging line is attached. Some fishermen and decoy makers prefer multiple line attachments and make them by drilling a series of holes in a *metal strip* they insert in the decoy, or by attaching a *wire* with a series of pigtail loops.

Many fishermen believe that the *eyes* are very important in luring a fish to an artificial bait. Ice fishermen are no different.

You may want to use an assortment of line attachments: (clockwise from top left) a cotter pin, metal strips, screw eyes, and a wire with pigtail loops.

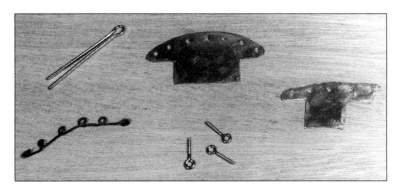

Simply painting the eyes onto a fish decoy is generally not enough. A variety of *tacks* and *nails* with substantial heads on them serve well, as do *plastic doll eyes* sold at craft and hobby shops. *Glass fish eyes* that look just like the real thing are available from taxidermy-supply houses if realism is what you want.

I personally prefer to punch *metal eyes* for my decoys from the same metal I use for the fins and tail, paint a black dot in each center to represent the pupil, and solder a wire pin on the back to attach them.

Glue. There are numerous ways to attach the fins, tail, and eyes to your decoy—and many of these will be presented later—but glueing them in place with a tough, waterproof glue is one of the methods. The glue I use for this purpose is *urethane glue.* Other glues, such as *epoxy* and *contact cement*, will also do the job. Although a little messy if handled without care, urethane glue is both tough and impervious to water, which makes it ideal for fish decoys. Be cautious, however, when using any glue. Protect your skin by wearing a pair of thin, tight-fitting surgical gloves.

Lead. To make your decoy sink in the water and have the proper swimming action, you'll need to fill its belly with molten lead. Most scrap metal dealers sell thin *lead sheets* by the pound, as do plumbing-supply stores. But you can also use the old *wheel weights* your friendly garage or service station owner may be throwing out.

Sealers and primers. The process of weighting and balancing your decoy involves dipping it in a tub of water to check for proper swimming action as you add the lead. It's therefore advisable to seal the wood beforehand. There are a number of sealers you can use. Among them are *shellac, clear lacquer,* and *sanding sealers*.

Although a sealer isn't absolutely necessary, you'll want at least to prime your decoy before you paint it. I recommend covering it with white *gesso*, the same paint artists use to prime their canvases before painting. It gives you an ideal undercoat, regardless of the type of paint you're going to use and no matter how you apply it.

5

Patterns

Photos and descriptions of the decoys carved from the patterns in this chapter are presented in the color section. They can act as your carving and painting guide. But remember, fish decoys are functional, made and used to fool fish. Your own imagination and interpretation of any particular species may do that as well as a realistic model. If *you* like the way your decoy looks when it's finished, then you've done a good job.

The dotted lines on the body of each drawing indicate an option: those at the base of the tail show where you can cut the blank if you choose to attach a metal tail; those on the upper jaw and end of the tail indicate variations relative to the species whose pattern you're carving (explanations are included in the color section).

The dotted lines on the fins indicate where they should be bent in order to attach them to the body as seen in the color photos.

SMALL DECOYS

The patterns presented in this section (both body and fins) are actual-size patterns ready to use. I recommend that you transfer them onto a piece of stiff paper or cardboard, such as poster board, or thin pieces of plastic so that you don't have to worry about their tearing or losing their shape with repeated use.

The sides of plastic milk cartons are ideal for making good, long-lasting patterns. This material is translucent, so you can lay it over the patterns on the following pages and trace them directly onto it. Cut the patterns out with a pair of scissors and you're ready to work.

If you're using poster board or some other stiff cardboard, copy the patterns in the book by first tracing them onto a thin see-through piece of tracing paper, onion skin, or wrapping tissue. Cut them out of this paper (which is too flimsy to use repeatedly on your wood), trace them onto the cardboard, and cut your final patterns out of that.

Be sure to trace the lines for the gill covers and the marks for the eyes. Cut them open with a knife or razor blade so that you can draw through them onto your decoy.

The fin patterns presented with each decoy can be copied in the same manner. These designs look good and work well with their respective body patterns. However, feel free to interchange different fin patterns with different body patterns, especially with the side fins. And don't be afraid to alter these designs to suit your own fancy. Eventually, you'll probably want to design your own decoys.

The wooden blanks you'll cut from the patterns for the smaller decoys are designed for standard three-quarter-inch (1.9 cm) stock lumber. Actually, the one-inch (2.5 cm) thickness is better and gives these decoys a nice, full-bodied plumpness. But most one-inch (2.5 cm) finished lumber—as it's usually sold at lumber companies—is really only about three quarters (1.9 cm) of an inch thick. Don't worry about that quarter inch (.64 cm) or so; use whatever is available. A decoy that's a little fatter or a little thinner than you'd like probably won't make any difference to a fish.

If you're a novice woodcarver or someone carving fish decoys for the first time, I suggest you carve some of the decoys in this section before moving on to those in the next. These decoys are smaller, less intricate, and more practical in their design. They'll therefore not take as long to complete. And I believe the best way to improve as a decoy carver is to make many decoys and get better through practice. Don't expect your first effort to produce a masterpiece. I also suggest you opt for a metal rather than a wooden tail on your first decoy, because a wooden tail can sometimes cause problems you don't need when you're just starting out.

Don't let beginner mistakes slow you down; work through them and try to avoid them the next time. Develop a feel for your tools and materials by carving several decoys. Later on you'll find it interesting to look back at your early efforts and compare them with your latest. You'll be pleasantly surprised by the improvement you've made along the way.

Patterns for the small decoys begin on the next page.

Small Trout

Small Perch

Small Bass

Small Sucker

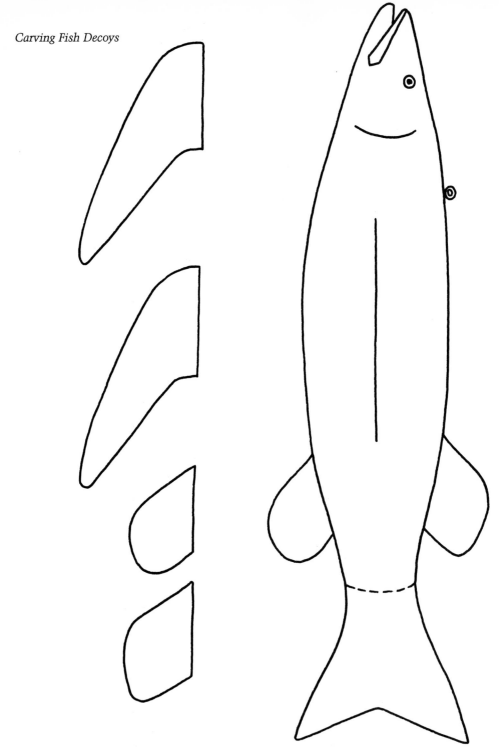

Small Pike and Musky

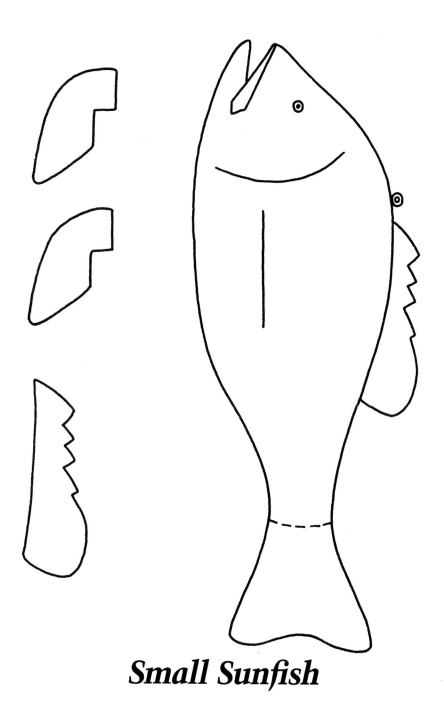

Small Sunfish

Frog

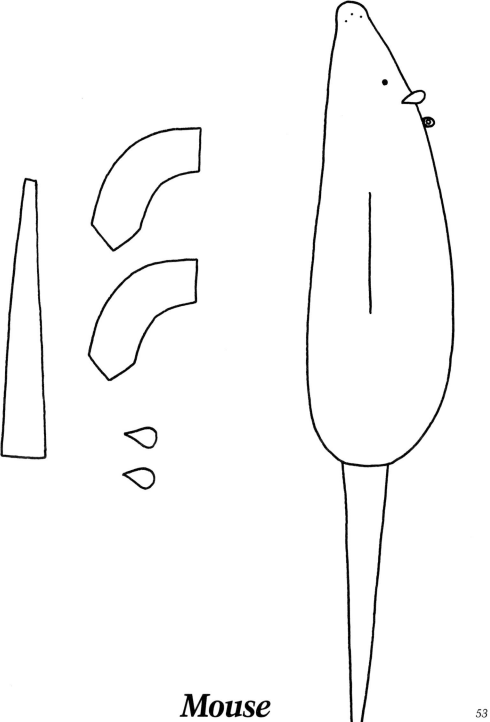

Mouse

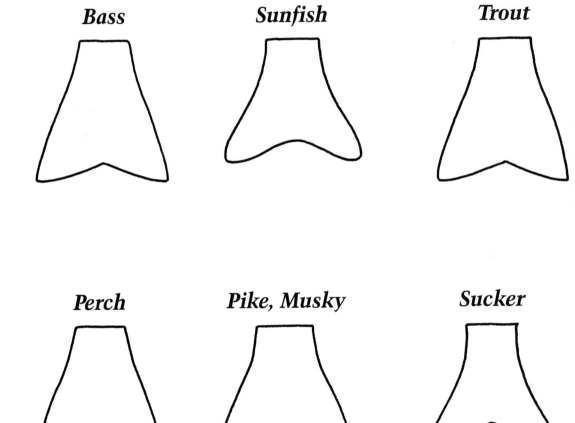

Bass   **Sunfish**   **Trout**

Perch   **Pike, Musky**   **Sucker**

Tails for Small Decoys

LARGE DECOYS

All patterns in the following section (body and fins) are seventy-four percent of their normal size and must be increased by thirty-five percent before you use them. This can be done with a photocopier that has enlarging capabilities, a scaling device used by graphic designers, a craft projector, or an overhead projector. (The formula to determine the full size is length of pattern ÷ 74 × 100 = full size of decoy.) As with the smaller decoys in the preceding section, the side fins shown with each of the following patterns are my personal preference and may be interchanged with those from other decoys.

Once you've enlarged the drawings to full size, make your working patterns as I explained with the smaller decoys. It may save you some time later if you mark not only the gill covers and eyes but also the fin placement, which you can transfer onto your carved decoy.

The ideal thickness of wood for these decoys is one and one half inches (3.8 cm). This thickness isn't always easy to come by. You can get thicker stock and cut it down, or you can glue two three-quarter-inch (1.9 cm) boards together, provided you use a waterproof glue and clamp the wood tightly.

If you're interested in anatomical accuracy, don't hesitate to consult a fish book as a reference. Or, if you want the real thing, either go fishing or visit your local fish market and get yourself a true model. Freeze it and pull it out now and then for study.

Rainbow Trout, Brook Trout, Brown Trout, and Lake Trout

Perch

Smallmouth Bass and Largemouth Bass

Sucker

Pike, Tiger Musky, and Great Lakes Musky

Sunfish

Walleye

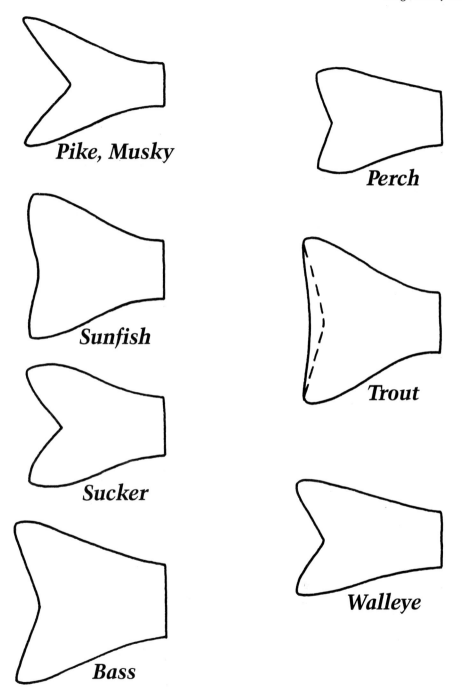

Pike, Musky

Perch

Sunfish

Trout

Sucker

Bass

Walleye

Tails for Large Decoys

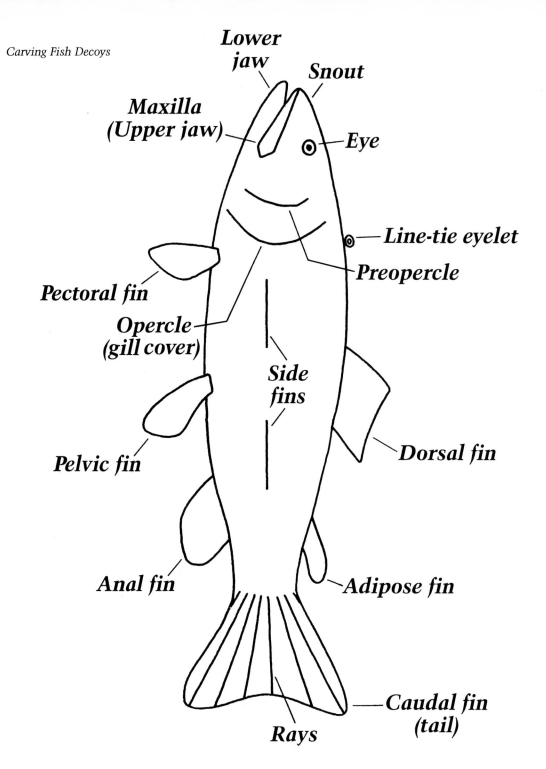

Lower jaw

Snout

Maxilla (Upper jaw)

Eye

Line-tie eyelet

Preopercle

Pectoral fin

Opercle (gill cover)

Side fins

Dorsal fin

Pelvic fin

Anal fin

Adipose fin

Rays

Caudal fin (tail)

Fish Decoy Anatomy

6

The Body

Begin carving your decoy by finding yourself a comfortable place to work and deciding on the tools, wood, and patterns you're going to use. Read through the text carefully. The photos that begin on p. 74 can be used as a reference when you sit down to carve.

CUTTING OUT THE BLANK

Lay your pattern on the wood so that it runs lengthwise with the grain, being sure to choose the nicest-looking spot where there are no knots and where the grain is tight and regular. Remember to use stock that is three quarters of an inch (1.9 cm) or one inch (2.5 cm) thick for the smaller decoys and one and one-half inches (3.8 cm) thick for the larger ones.

Saw out the blank with a coping saw or band saw. If you work with a coping saw, use a vise or clamp to hold your wood firmly while you saw. This way, you'll be able to get a safe, even cut. If you use a band saw, cutting out your blank will be a snap. A scroll saw or jigsaw may also do the trick, provided it will handle the density and thickness of your wood.

Before you start carving your decoy, draw a centerline on the top and underside of the blank. This will orient you on the center while you carve and will help you to keep the body more symmetrical. It won't hurt to draw the entire shape of the decoy on the blank, either.

ROUGHING OUT THE BLANK

Now you're ready to begin roughing out your decoy. I like a drawknife for this purpose. I simply clamp the tail of my blank in a vise and begin shaping the body. I first work on the back, then turn it over and work on the belly. On the tail end, I narrow my blank down only to the base of the tail, because the tail itself is in the vise. Once I have the basic shape of my decoy-to-be, I remove it from the vise, draw the curve in the tail, and cut it with the band saw. If you don't rough out your decoy with a drawknife but use your carving knife instead, you should probably cut the curve in the tail when you cut out the blank.

The amount of curve you put in the tail will determine, to a great degree, the radius of the circle your decoy will make in the water, although it will also depend somewhat on the weight of your decoy: the lighter the decoy, the more control you'll have manipulating it in the water. A heavy decoy will do pretty much what the curve of the tail dictates. You'll have to do some guessing about the turn of the tail until you get to know your decoys, but start out giving it only about a 20-degree turn. Or better yet, start out with a metal-tail decoy that you can adjust as you learn how much curve you like.

Many fishermen and decoy carvers opt for the metal tail because it allows them to alter the action of their decoy by simply bending the tail one way or the other. If you choose to carve a decoy with a metal tail, you should cut the slot for it when you cut out your blank. The slot should be cut on the centerline nearly three quarters of an inch (1.9 cm) into the body and just a little wider than the thickness of the metal you're using.

REFINING THE BLANK

You can now carve the final shape of your decoy with carving knives. I personally prefer to work first with a larger Swedish-style knife, then with my smaller chip-carving knife for the detail. But I'll often alternate between the two.

As you carve, turn your blank over often and try to take equal amounts of wood off each side. Let the lines you've drawn guide you. Hold the blank up in front of you every now and then and turn it around to check for symmetry. Carve in this manner until you're satisfied with its shape.

At this point, you'll need to make a decision about whether to sand your decoy. I prefer not to sand mine except for the tail, because I like the uneven surface the carve marks leave. If the knife is razor-sharp, the body will be as smooth as when it's sanded anyway. The carve marks on the finished decoy, I believe, make it clear that these are in fact wooden fish carved by hand with no pretenses to be anything other than that. Let nature do her work and you do yours; there's no need for competition.

The carve marks could have a practical function as well, for they appear to give the decoy a sense of strength and movement, and their flat, many-angled surfaces are a little like prisms that reflect light in every direction. These eye-catching reflections probably look quite interesting to a curious pike or musky.

SANDING

Even if you decide to leave the carve marks on the body of your decoy, you'll probably have to sand a small area at the base of the tail where it meets the body, because the inside of the curve is difficult to carve smooth with a knife. Use a piece of medium- or fine-grit sandpaper. You might find it helpful to make yourself a sanding stick for this purpose by glueing sandpaper around a three-eighths- or half-inch (.95 or 1.3 cm) dowel.

If you decide to burn lines representing rays in the tail, which I usually do, sand the entire tail smooth. You can use your sanding stick and a small piece of sandpaper here. But if you have a small sanding drum for your drill or flexible shaft grinder, use it. It will make this task much easier.

If you're a person who prefers a decoy with a smooth, even surface, or if you plan to texture it in some way, then you should probably sand the whole body smooth at this juncture. Begin with medium-grit sandpaper and finish with fine-grit. But again, you may want to use your drill and sanding drum instead — at least to begin with — and finish up by hand.

Before going on to the section on detailing, I must include a special note of advice about carving the tail. Instead of carving it to its final shape before you add detail on the body of your decoy, wait until afterward. You'll no doubt be bracing it against your body, and there's a chance of breaking it. Or, you may want to leave the tail a quarter-inch (.64 cm) thick, even at the end, as did many of the old-time carvers. This will make it stronger and more practical to use.

DETAILING

No matter what you decide to do with the body surface of your decoy, you'll probably want to add some detail to it. This isn't absolutely necessary, however, and won't add or detract from the action of your decoy. But it will add realism and charm, probably making it more attractive to both fish and fisherman.

How far you go with the detail is a matter of personal choice. Beyond a point, painstakingly careful renditions of scales will matter only to you, not to the fish. Even if your decoy will spend more time ornamenting the mantel than swimming beneath the ice, you may still want to capture the primitive look of the old-time working decoys. I find fish decoys carved and painted with wild imagination just as appealing as, if not more than, those that are made to look like the real thing down to the most minute details.

Keeping that in mind, let's look first at some basic detail that I like to add to my decoys, especially the larger ones, and then I'll suggest some additional things you can do. If you really want to challenge Mother Nature, I'll give you some advice on how you might do that, too.

The head. On my smaller decoys, I add eyes, the upper jaw (maxilla), and gill covers (opercles). On the larger ones, I not only add the eyes and upper jaw, but also carve the gill covers to stand out from the sides. I also make a cut in each cheek to represent the preopercles.

On some fish, the upper jaw extends beyond the eyes. On others, it stops below or short of them. I take this into account, especially with the larger decoys. On the other hand, I don't usually round the ends of the upper jaw as they are on the real fish. I simply cut them in a V shape instead, which is nothing more than a stylistic characteristic I picked up and don't feel like changing. What you do is strictly personal.

Carving the gill covers and upper jaw is a little like chip carving, and your chip-carving knife or jackknife is ideal. If such detail carving is new to you, and you're a little reluctant, practice on a scrap piece of wood to build up confidence before starting on your decoy.

All the detail you plan to add to your carving should be drawn on your pattern first. This gives you a clearer idea of how it will look on the decoy. If you then cut through the lines with a knife or razor blade and trace the detail onto the wood, it will be easier to match both sides. It's especially helpful to do this with the eyes and gill covers, but you may also mark the upper jaw, tail rays, and fins this way. Be sure that when you cut these lines in your pattern, you stop short of cutting the pattern apart and ruining it. I generally mark only the eyes and gill covers through my pattern, but if I'm planning to burn in fins, I mark them too. It's just as easy to draw the upper jaw without the pattern as it is with it. The gill-cover lines must also be completed; continue them until they meet under the jaw.

Lay your pattern on one side of your decoy. Push it against a pencil held at the mouth opening of both the pattern and the decoy until they line up. Draw the markings, first on one side, then the other. These lines on the wood act only as a reference, because you'll have to adjust them and complete them later without the pattern. Be sure to line up the eyes with each other and mark their spots clearly. This will give you a reference point for the upper jaw, which you should draw next.

When you're ready to carve the detail, begin with the preopercle line on the cheek. Hold your knife perpendicular to the side of your decoy with the cutting edge of the blade angled down about 45 degrees. Follow the pencil line with the tip of your knife blade and make a cut along it about one-eighth inch (.32 cm) deep. If you don't cut deep enough the first time, go over it again.

Now, with your knife at about a 45 degree angle to the cut you first made, leaning the handle toward the tail, cut along this line about one-eighth inch (.32 cm) away from it. If you do it right and make this cut deep enough to meet the first cut you made, the result will be a clean, shallow channel that represents the pre-opercle. But if you don't get it clean on the first cut, go over it until you do.

Next, with the same basic method described above, cut along the lines you drew for the upper jaw, making the depth of your first cut only about one sixteenth of an inch (.16 cm). The result this time will be an upper jaw that stands out slightly from the head. Be extra careful cutting the upper jaw. This is very delicate work. If you should happen to take out an unexpected chip, fill it in with wood filler and carve it when it's hard.

Finally, carve the gill covers so that they look as if they're slightly open, about one eighth of an inch (.32 cm). This time, instead of making the first cut perpendicularly along the lines you drew as the edge of the gill covers, lean your knife just slightly toward the tail. This will reinforce the effect of open covers. Make a second cut (about 45 degrees) to clear away an eighth-inch (.32 cm) channel around the gill covers.

To make the head stand out even more, bevel the sides of your decoy into the base of the gill covers, starting about one inch (2.5 cm) behind them. As you do this, hold your decoy out in front of you now and then to make sure you're keeping the body relatively even on both sides. Then, if you sanded the body, finish up by resanding the areas you just carved.

The tail and fins. A woodburning pen is not a big investment and is excellent for adding detail to your decoy. You can purchase a good, reliable Dremel-brand pen for as little as $19. It comes with a standard V-shaped tip that will serve most, if not all, of your needs. The Hot Tool is another reasonably priced pen set that is popular among bird carvers. It comes with an assortment of tips as well as a control that allows you to regulate the temperature of the tip. This is helpful if you plan to do especially fine detailing. Woodburning pens that cost hundreds of dollars are also available, but are probably more than you'll ever need for fish decoys.

I use the woodburning pen primarily for adding rays on a wooden tail and occasionally for burning in pectoral and pelvic fins on the sides of my decoys.

Before setting the woodburning pen to your decoy, sand the tail to its final shape and draw the rays on it with a pencil. Trace them through your pattern if you like, but they're just as easy to draw without it. The best way to get an even, fanlike spread is to start with the centerline and move out in both directions from there. Draw the rays on both sides of the tail so that they match up at the outer edge. Then burn them in, but only about one sixteenth of an inch (.16 cm) deep.

You'll be surprised at how much life and sense of movement just a few shallow lines give to a wooden fish. And if you want to add even more life to your decoy, you can use your knife or a small carving chisel to make the alternate soft and spiny rays even more prominent.

As far as the pectoral and pelvic fins go, I usually cut them out of metal and attach them to my decoy by either glueing them in or screwing them on, which is explained in Chapter 10. Occasionally, I decide to depict these fins by burning them into the sides of my decoy, painting them later so that they stand out even more.

To match these fins on each side of the decoy, draw them on your pattern and cut them out, leaving a clearly defined hole where they were. Again, lay your pattern on the side of your decoy, line it up, and draw the fins on the wood. Add a few lines for the rays, then burn in both the outline and the rays with your burning pen.

Some carvers use another technique, which is a little like relief carving, to depict these fins. Instead of simply outlining them, as described above, they carve the wood away from the outer edges, leaving them raised about an eighth of an inch (.32 cm) from the body. Final touches are added by either carving or burning in the rays and painting the fins.

The scales. The last and most extravagant aspect of detailing is texturing the body to create a scalelike effect. As stated earlier, I prefer not to sand the body of my decoys but feel that the carve marks themselves create a sense of naturalness in the decoy and help keep it within the limits of the simple nature and origins of the craft and sport. But many decoy carvers attempt to depict each and every scale down to the last detail, and others create scalelike appearances that are more abstract than exact.

If you want to be exact, you can go so far as to research how many scales your particular species of decoy should have along the lateral line, draw the correct number on each side, and burn or carve them in one by one. This is a time-consuming task, but if you see it as a challenge and will be pleased with the effect, go ahead and do it.

However, there are less tedious ways to give the impression of scales on your decoy. For example, you can simply draw lines on the sides in a criss-cross fashion and go over them with your knife or woodburning pen to create a simple cross-hatching effect.

You can also create a scalelike effect with a small gouge by lightly tapping it straight into the sides of your decoy, leaving a curved impression in the wood that looks like the edge of a scale. If you make many rows of these marks from the gill covers to the tail, they may create the effect you like.

You can use this same gouge to dig a number of small, short grooves into the sides of your decoy either in a random order or in rows that look more like scales.

A very simple method that also gives your decoy a scaly look consists of using a coarse wood rasp to scratch and rough up the sides. This leaves marks that are similar to the cross-hatching described above but more random and subtle.

Power carvers with various grinding wheels will also give you texturing that looks like scales. And netting made specifically for painting scales on fishing plugs and lures can be ordered from tackle suppliers.

So, as you see, there is no lack of texturing ideas if you decide you want to embellish the body of your decoy.

SEALING AND PRIMING

When you've completed all the detailing, you're ready to set your carving aside for a while and go on to other tasks. But before you do, seal the wood for leading and painting.

I use gesso, which is a white acrylic paint that artists use to prime their canvases before painting. Gesso is a water-based paint that doesn't really seal your wood, but it gives you a nice undercoat to paint over. Some woods you use, such as basswood, may tend to get fuzzy when you apply gesso directly to them. If this happens, simply sand the surface and give it another coat.

One way to avoid fuzziness and seal your wood better is to brush or spray a sealer directly on the wood before applying gesso. The old standby, shellac, can be used as well as such faster-drying sealers as clear lacquer or sanding sealer. No matter what you use, sand the surface smooth with extra-fine sandpaper or steel wool when it's dry.

You can paint directly over these sealers without a primer if you like, but I recommend covering them with a coat of gesso first. And it's best to do that now, before you weight and balance your decoy with lead. You can, however, wait until just before you actually paint it.

Besides the sealers I've mentioned here, you may want to try some of the paint primers that are available in spray cans. They come in an assortment of colors and may give you a special effect you'll like when your decoy is painted. Whenever you try something new, however, experiment on a scrap piece of wood before trying it on a decoy you've spent hours carving.

HOLLOWING OUT THE BELLY

Before setting your decoy aside to start working on the fins, you should hollow out the belly, which you'll later fill with lead for weight and balance. Be sure the sealer and primer are thoroughly dry so that you don't have to worry about the chips and dust from the cavity getting stuck to them.

Begin by drawing two lines on the belly about a quarter-inch (.64 cm) apart from just behind the gill covers to just before the spot where you'll place the anal fin. Be sure the space between these two lines is centered, then dig it out just slightly over halfway through to the back of your decoy.

There are actually a couple of ways to hollow out the stomach cavity. The traditional method is simply to use your carving knife, and maybe a small gouge or chisel, to cut and dig until the area is clear. This can be a tough, time-consuming job that's done more easily with an electric drill or, better yet, a drill press.

If you have a drill or drill press, get yourself a quarter-inch (.64 cm) brad point bit. You can use a standard quarter-inch (.64 cm) bit, but the brad point won't jump around on the wood as a standard bit tends to do. This will allow you to be more precise with your cuts. A Forstner bit is also more accurate than a standard drill bit.

Drill the holes next to each other, as close as possible, between the two lines you drew on the belly from the gill covers to the anal fin. The depth of the holes should be just slightly over halfway through to the back. If wood remains between the holes when you've drilled all of them, clear it away with your knife. You can actually clear the cavity by running the drill bit back and forth in it.

Before leaving this section, I must include a special note about hollowing out your decoy if you're attaching a metal tail. As mentioned earlier, metal fins add weight to the decoy, and if you're using heavy metal, you may find that your decoy becomes tail-heavy when you add just a small amount of lead to the belly cavity. To avoid this problem, which is especially noticeable with the small decoys, start the cavity as far forward as possible (nearly under the eyes), and don't let it extend much beyond half the length of the body. Dig it a little deeper than usual where possible.

Now, with your decoy sealed and primed, and the belly hollowed out, you can leave it alone for a while and move on to making the fins and eyes. You can also cut out a metal tail if you chose not to carve a wooden one as part of the body.

Use a piece of thin cardboard or plastic for your pattern. Trace it onto the wood so that it runs lengthwise with the grain.

After tracing my pattern onto the wood, I cut it out with the band saw. I also cut out the mouth at this time.

The blank is held by the tail in a vise as I rough out my decoy with a drawknife, which can be both pulled and pushed over the wood.

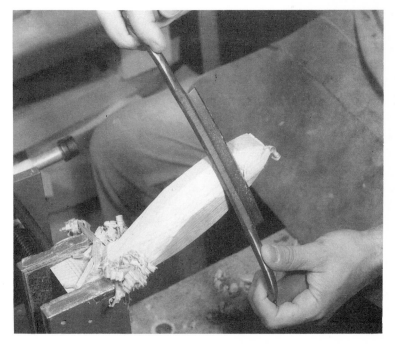

I draw a curve in the tail (approximately 20 degrees). Whether the tail turns to the left or right really doesn't matter; curve it in the direction that is most compatible with the grain.

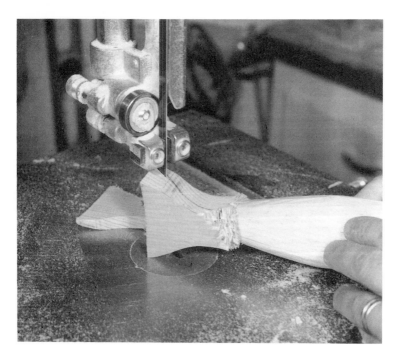

The curve in the tail can be cut with a coping saw, scroll saw, or a band saw as I do here. I find it best to cut the inside of the curve first.

If you decide to go with a metal tail, cut the slot at the same time you cut out the blank. It should be centered and cut about three quarters of an inch (1.9 cm) deep.

Instead of sanding my decoys, I use my knife to shave the surface smooth. This leaves an uneven, natural-looking surface that adds life to the decoy.

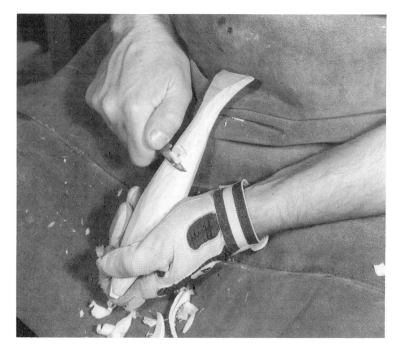

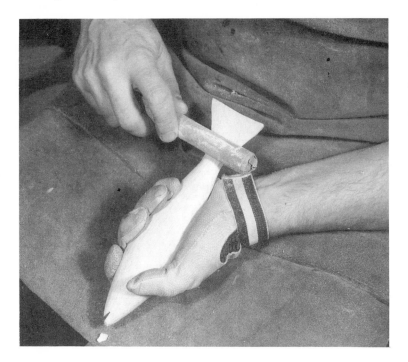

The base of the tail, and often the tail itself, are the only areas on the decoy that I sand. Here, I use a half-inch (1.3 cm) dowel wrapped with sandpaper as a sanding stick.

A sanding drum on a drill simplifies the task of shaping the tail. A smooth surface makes it easier to add detail lines.

Cut detail lines through the pattern so that they can be traced onto the carving.

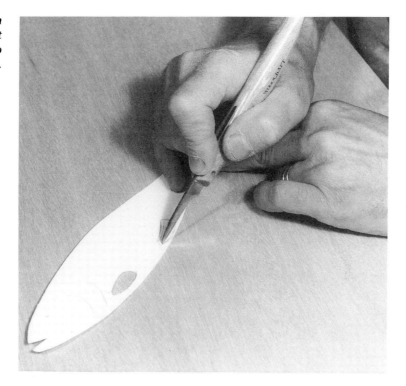

To match the detail markings on each side of the decoy, position the pattern against a pencil held in the mouth opening.

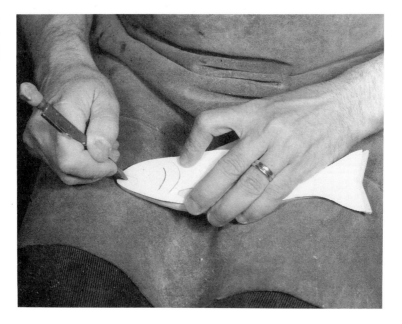

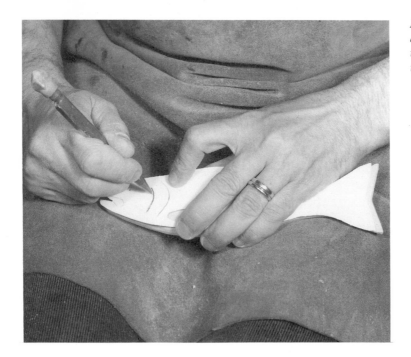

Hold the pattern in place and draw the detail lines through the openings onto the decoy.

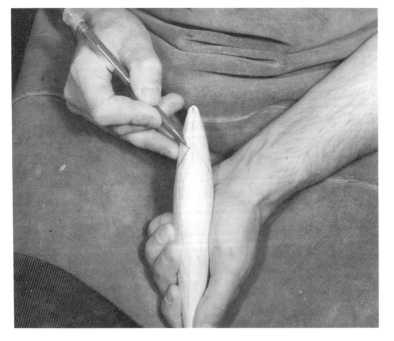

After I've drawn as much as I can through the pattern, I remove it from the blank and adjust and complete the markings. Note the centerline on the lower jaw; this helps to match the gill covers.

It's just as easy to draw the upper jaw freehand as it is to trace it through the pattern. On some fish, it extends past the eye. On others, such as the rainbow trout, it stops at the eye. I usually draw the end of the upper jaw in a **V**-shape, not rounded as it is on a real fish.

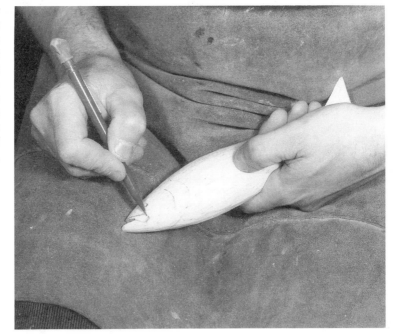

The preopercle line is a good place to start carving the detail. Here, after making a cut along the pencil mark, I make a second cut at a 45-degree angle to the first. This leaves a shallow channel on the gill cover that represents the preopercle.

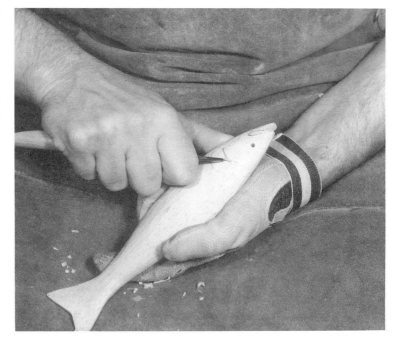

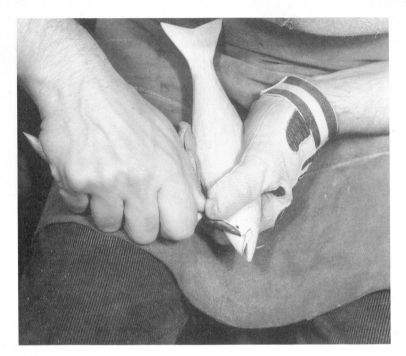

Trim the wood away from around the upper jaw with the tip of the knife blade.

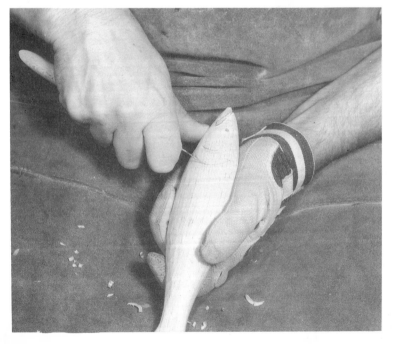

I make a slightly angled cut an eighth-inch (.32 cm) deep along the gill-cover line with the point of my knife.

Clear the wood away from the gill cover to give it the appearance of being open.

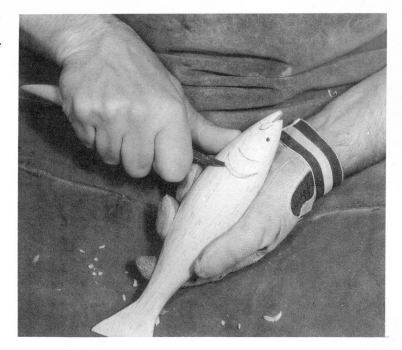

Bevel the body toward the gill covers starting about an inch (2.5 cm) away. This will make the head more prominent.

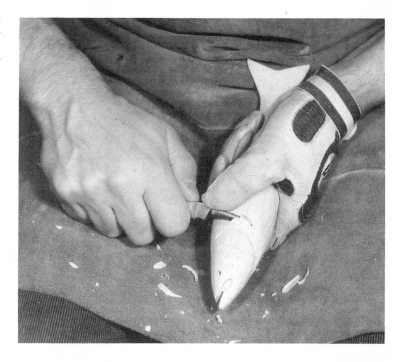

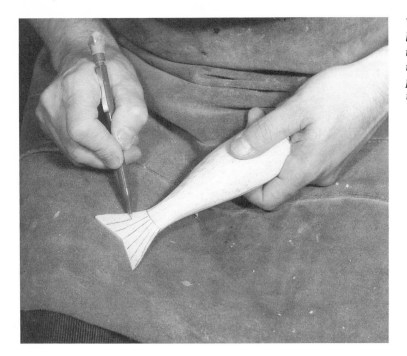

When drawing the rays, begin with a line across the base of the tail. Draw the center ray first and proceed outward from there.

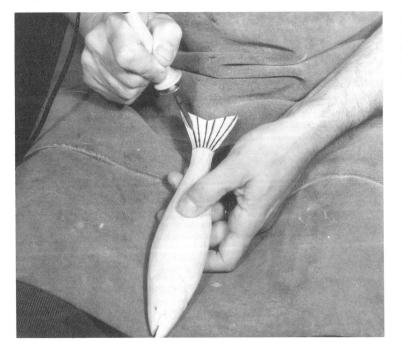

Burning rays in the tail is a simple task, but they may also be carved with a knife or small carving chisel.

Fins have been burned into the side of this sucker and then painted. As seen here, a fish decoy out of the water will hang with its tail lower than the head. In the water, it should float nearly parallel to the lake bottom.

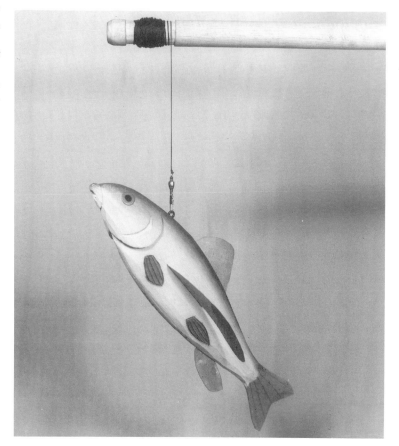

Texturing the body of a fish decoy can be done in a number of ways: (from top to bottom) scales pressed in with a small gouge; cross-hatching done with a burning pen; shallow indentations made with a gouge; a scale pattern made with a burning pen. The tail rays on the top and bottom fish are carved rather than burned.

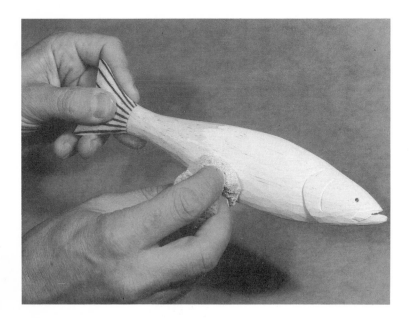

Applying gesso with a sponge. This offers an excellent primer to paint over.

Draw a slot a quarter-inch (.64 cm) wide on the belly from the gill covers to the anal fin. Hollowed out, this will provide a cavity for the lead.

I hollow out the belly from the gill covers to the anal fin and about half-way through the decoy with a quarter-inch (.64 cm) bit in the drill press.

7

Fins, Line-Tie, and Eyes

FINS

Metal. The fins for fish decoys can be fashioned from a variety of materials, but the most common and practical is metal.

There are a number of reasons why decoy carvers and fishermen prefer metal fins. First of all, just about any kind of metal can be used, and has been used, as long as it's fairly easy to cut with tin snips or shears. It's not hard to find tin cans, old stovepipes, pieces of brass, copper, or galvanized metal, all of which are commonly used.

Second, when fins fashioned from these metals are properly attached to the wooden body, they're sturdier than fins cut from other materials and will take quite a bit of abuse both in and out of the water. This means they'll hold up well for many fishing seasons.

Third, metal fins add weight to a decoy, which is desirable, because fish decoys have to be able to sink.

Finally, the metal that decoy carvers use for fins is almost always flexible and can be bent to alter the swimming patterns of a decoy while the fisherman is in the shanty. Not only the tail, but also the side fins (either attached in pairs or singly to each side and sometimes the belly) create variations in a decoy's swimming patterns when turned this way or that; they can speed it up, slow it down, or cause it to swim in the manner of an injured fish.

These are some of the reasons I prefer metal fins—brass and copper in particular. Besides being practical, these metals look good on a finished decoy and add color and flash in the water. I purchase my materials from scrap-metal dealers, but many hobby shops and jewelry-supply houses carry them as well.

I sometimes use galvanized sheet metal or tin. Although it's very sturdy and easy to work with, it doesn't add the attraction in the water that brass and copper do. In fact, when I use these metals, I generally paint the fins as part of the color scheme of the body.

Once you've decided on the metal you want to use, cut a piece large enough for all the fins on the decoy you've just carved. Clean and buff the metal to give it a nice, even finish, then lay your fin patterns on it. Trace them with a pencil or felt pen and cut them out with your tin snips or metal shears. I use a pair of fine metal-cutters called plate shears. They have curved blades that allow me to make very tight turns, which is essential for cutting

I draw trout fins on a piece of copper after it has been cleaned with steel wool. Copper and brass make attractive fins when left unpainted.

Cutting metal fins is not difficult with a good pair of shears.

fins, especially spiny-rayed dorsal fins like those on sunfish, perch, and bass.

You can also cut out your fins with a jeweler's saw or coping saw fitted with a fine, metal-cutting blade. In fact, you may prefer to use a saw, because it leaves your fins flatter than when you cut them with shears. This means you don't necessarily have to hammer them unless you want to add texture.

If you do cut out your fins with shears, you'll have to pound them flat before attaching them to your decoy. This is where you'll need an anvil of some type to hammer on. I simply use an old piece of steel plating I picked up at the scrapyard. But a piece of angle iron, the top of your vise, or any hard metal surface will do. Even a small block of very hard wood will suffice.

The hammer you use to pound your fins is going to determine their surface texture. If you want the metal to have a smooth surface, you should use a plastic or rawhide mallet, because a steel hammer will leave hammer marks on the metal. This, however, is actually the effect I like to achieve. It gives the fins a mottled look and creates an uneven surface that will reflect light

The fins will have to be flattened if you cut them out with metal shears. I like to create a mottled finish on my fins with a heavy hammer. A plastic or rawhide mallet will leave them smooth.

at a multitude of angles in the water, just like the carve marks left on the body. For even more mottling, you may want to use a ball peen hammer.

One of the reasons I like copper and brass is that their color can be easily altered to produce many different effects. They can be buffed to a high luster and lacquered to keep them that way, or they can be left raw to tarnish and change character naturally over time. I usually dip them in a liver of sulphur solution (which I'll explain in Chapter 10) to get the effect I like.

Once you've hammered your fins flat, you're ready to attach them to the decoy. This can be done in a number of ways. Many decoy carvers design the side fins with a long tab that reaches into the middle of the body. They place them so that they can be inserted into a slot in the side of the body where the cavity for the lead has been made and then stick the tabs through these slots all the way into the cavity before leading the decoy.

The side fins on this trout are attached with screws. The tab was bent at a 90-degree angle, and two holes were drilled for the screws. The metal fins are painted, and the eyes, pectoral fins, and pelvic fins are burned in. The tail rays were made with a small carving chisel.

It is essential that all the fins are on your decoy when you weight and balance it, but with the tabs in the cavity, this means they'll be permanently affixed once the lead hardens. This is probably the surest way to attach the side fins, but when you paint your decoy, you must either work around them or paint them along with the body.

There are other ways to attach the side fins permanently *after* the leading process. One way is to screw them into the decoy with small screws. Do this by bending each tab at a right angle where it meets the body of the fin. Drill two small holes through the tabs and screw the fins in place. Or attach them to the belly of the decoy by designing each one as a single piece of metal that reaches across the body. Drill a hole in the center and screw them onto the belly.

The metal tail can also be screwed on once it has been set in the slot you cut for it earlier. If you do this to supplement the glue, you'll make sure the tail doesn't fall out if it gets banged around. I'll discuss the glues and glueing procedures in Chapter 10, because you need to attach the fins only temporarily before weighting and balancing your decoy with lead.

If you're going to glue the fins in place but not paint them, you should insert them at this point without the glue. You'll want to pull them out after you've leaded your decoy so that you won't

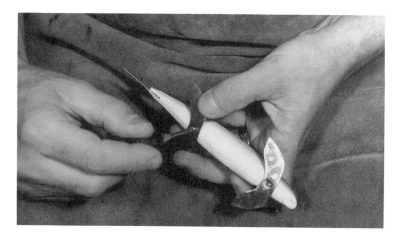

It's not uncommon to attach the floating fins to the belly of a decoy, as I do here with this small sucker.

have to worry about them while painting the body. When you've finished painting your decoy and the final coat is dry, then glue them in permanently.

Begin setting the fins in place by drawing a centerline on the back of your decoy for the dorsal fin and then on the underside for the anal fin, if you choose to add one. Set the dorsal fin in the correct spot along the centerline on the back and press it into the wood, leaving marks where you want to insert it. Cut a slot for the fin about a quarter-inch (.64 cm) deep with your carving knife or jackknife, and insert the fin. Set all your fins in place in this same manner, making sure they line up on both sides. The easiest way to line up the side, pectoral, and pelvic fins is to insert them one at a time. Hold the decoy at eye level in front of you, line up the opposing fin with the inserted one, and mark the spot by pressing the fin into the wood. Then cut the slot as described above.

If you plan to paint the fins along with the body, you might as well glue them in place now. Be sure to give the glue a chance to dry before you start the leading process. And if you're inserting the side fins into the belly cavity to embed them in the lead, place them in their permanent position at this time. Otherwise, you'll remove them after balancing to allow for ease in painting.

Leather. Not all decoy carvers fashion their fins from metal. Leather is used often and serves very well. Leather fins can be shaped to vary the action of the decoy and, some believe, create a

Draw a line for the dorsal fin centered on the back. Do the same on the underside for the anal fin. Note that the trout also needs a line for the adipose fin.

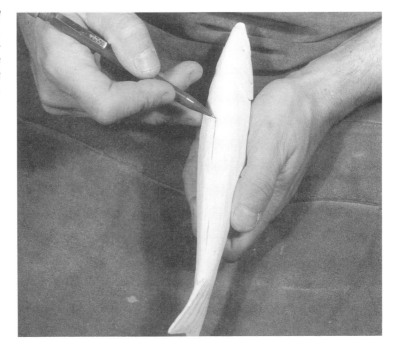

Mark the placement of the fin along the centerline by pressing it into the wood, leaving a slight indentation.

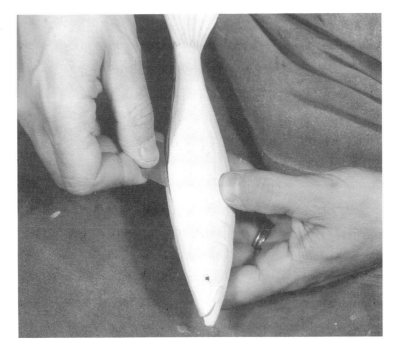

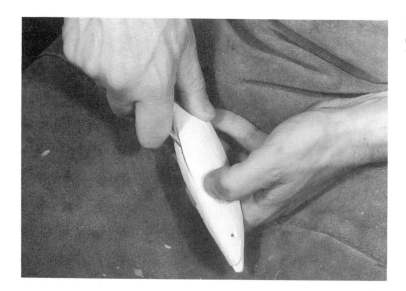

Cut a slot a quarter-inch (.64 cm) deep for the fins with your knife.

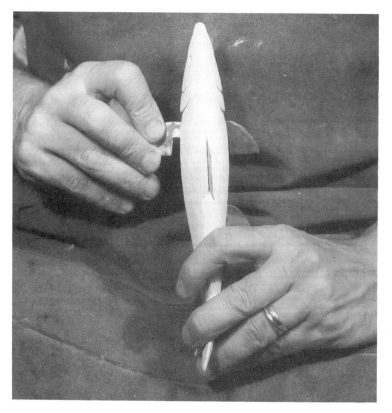

Be sure the side fins line up with each other. This can be done by looking straight into the nose of the decoy as I am doing here. Once you find the correct spot, mark it with the fin.

Cut a slot for the pelvic fins by inserting the knife blade into the belly. Use the thinnest blade available so that you don't split the wood along the empty cavity.

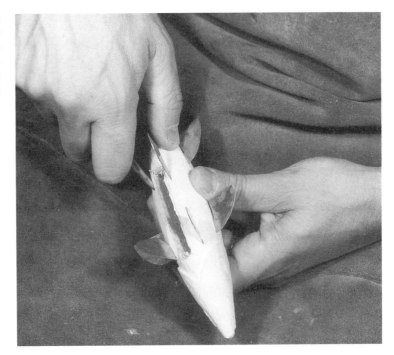

softer, more natural look to a decoy. They can be cut from an old belt, purse, jacket, or pair of boots or shoes, so the material isn't hard to find. And leather isn't difficult to cut, either. A knife or a pair of scissors will do the job. Leather fins are a little more difficult to attach, however, due to their bulk. Glueing them in place is the best approach.

The primary drawback with leather fins is that they usually won't hold up as long as metal fins. Leather has a tendency to crack and rot when repeatedly immersed in water, so these fins often break off while the body of the decoy is still in good condition. That's one of the reasons it's not common to find old decoys with their original leather fins. Another possible drawback of leather is that it doesn't really add weight to the decoy as does metal.

Wood. Except for the tail, which is very commonly carved as part of the body, wood is not the material of choice when you're making fins. Although wooden fins may look good on a decoy, and can be elaborately carved and textured, they're rather impractical.

First of all, wooden fins add unwanted buoyancy. Second, if carved as one piece with the body—which can be done for the tail, dorsal, adipose, and anal fins—they break too easily even with careful treatment. And finally, wooden side fins are more difficult to attach than other types of fins, can't be adjusted, and often break off right in the fisherman's tackle bag.

There are still other materials that you can use for fins, such as plastic or rubber, which a few carvers do use. But when all the choices are considered, your best bet is to stick with metal.

LINE-TIE

Once you have your fins in place, you're just about ready to weight and balance your decoy. But to do this, you'll need to attach a line-tie eyelet to the back, just behind the head. And this is as good a time as any to do it.

Screw eye. The simplest, and perhaps the best, line-tie is a small screw eye like those found on older fishing plugs. I like to use a five-eighths inch (1.6 cm) screw eye with .063-inch (.16 cm) wire diameter, which can be ordered from Netcraft, a tackle-supply house listed in the appendix. This size is long enough to hold under any normal fishing conditions. Smaller screw eyes may pull out when your decoy has been in the water all day and

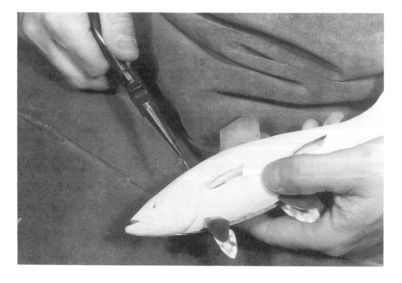

Place the line-tie eyelet a quarter of the way from the nose to the tail.

A multiple line-tie cut from a piece of metal must have an extra-long tab that is inserted well into the back of the decoy. Glue it in place, and secure it further by setting a small nail into a hole drilled through the decoy and the tab.

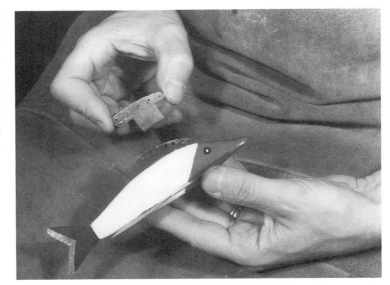

the wood has softened somewhat. The smallest screw eyes you'll find at the hardware store will also do.

Just where you place this line-tie eyelet along the center-line on the back will affect the swimming action of your decoy. I find that a quarter of the way from the nose to the tail is pretty much a standard spot you can rely on for good swimming action, if you're attaching only one eyelet. However, many carvers and fishermen prefer multiple line-tie eyelets so that they can vary the swimming action of their decoys simply by attaching the jigging line to a different eyelet. Generally, the farther away from the snout you attach your line, the broader the circle your decoy will make when you jig it up. Conversely, it will make a tighter circle when the line is farther forward.

The easiest way to make multiple line-tie eyelets is simply to add two or three screw eyes about a quarter-inch (.64 cm) apart beginning a quarter of the way from the nose to the tail.

Metal strip. It's not uncommon to see decoys with a strip of metal running all the way from the head to the middle of the back with small holes drilled through it an eighth- to a quarter-inch (.32 to .64 cm) apart. This doubles as a multiple line-tie and dorsal fin. If you use this kind of line-tie, be sure to set it at least

99

half an inch (1.3 cm) into the back of your decoy. In addition to glueing it in, drill a hole through the back of the decoy into the base of the line-tie strip and run a pin or screw through it so that it won't pull out.

Pigtail wire. Another traditional way to make a multiple line-tie is to bend a series of pigtail loops about a quarter-inch (.64 cm) apart along a two-inch (5.1 cm) piece of sturdy wire. Attach this strip to your decoy by screwing it to the back through a loop made at each end of the wire.

Cotter pin. For an exceptionally strong line-tie eyelet, some decoy makers use cotter pins. The carver attaches the cotter pin to the decoy by first drilling a hole from the back into the lead cavity. He inserts the pin and bends it apart in the cavity so that it can't pull out. A small bit of putty or wood filler is stuffed into the hole around the pin to hold it in place and to seal the hole. When the decoy is filled with lead, the cotter pin is permanently embedded in the decoy and is as secure a line-tie as you'll find.

But when all the different line-ties are compared, the screw eye is probably the best choice. If it's long enough, it will be plenty strong. It's easy to attach, and you can make multiple line-ties simply by adding more screw eyes. (See Chapter 4 for a picture of the various line-tie possibilities.)

One alternative to these line-tie attachments is a small hole drilled through the body just behind the head near the top of the

Several pigtail loops in a piece of wire make a good line-tie. I wrap a wire around a nail driven into a piece of wood to get the loop I want. I'll also make a loop at each end of the wire so that I can attach it to the decoy with screws.

back. This was a method used last century by the Lake Chautauqua carvers in New York.

EYES

It always seems that a fish decoy is never really finished until the eyes are added. And even if they are no more than dots painted to look like eyes, they always seem to add the final touch that brings a decoy to life.

Glass. If realism is what you're trying to achieve in your decoy, you can order glass fish eyes from the taxidermy-supply houses listed in the appendix. If you use glass eyes, mount them by drilling a shallow hole just slightly larger than the eye itself, set them in, and fill around them with wood filler. Shape and sand the wood filler so that the eye and area around it look natural.

Metal. I personally prefer to make fish decoy eyes in a more traditional fashion by using nails and tacks, or by cutting circles from the same metal I selected for fins.

On the smaller decoys, I sometimes just paint eyes directly on the decoy by first laying down a white dot with an eraser on the

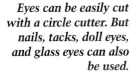

Eyes can be easily cut with a circle cutter. But nails, tacks, doll eyes, and glass eyes can also be used.

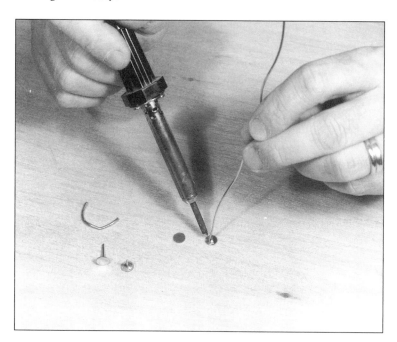

I solder an anchor wire to the back of the eye.

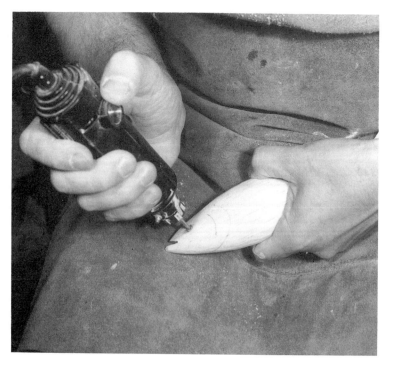

Drill eighth-inch (.32 cm) holes where you marked the eyes. Later, you'll insert the wire attached to the back of each eye and glue it in place.

end of a pencil. Then I use the point of the pencil to make a small, black dot in the center of the white one.

Inserting nails or carpet tacks for eyes not only adds character to your decoy, but also is in keeping with a long decoy-making tradition. And don't be afraid to experiment with different types of nails, thumbtacks, upholstery tacks, or whatever else you think will do the job.

The easiest way to attach these nails is first to cut them off so that they're no more than a quarter-inch (.64 cm) long, poke a hole with an awl or sharp nail where you had marked the eyes earlier, and push the tacks in with a pair of pliers. With harder wood, drill a small hole for the tack first, then glue it in. You should do this before you paint your decoy, because you'll want to paint these tacks in the same manner as I described above for painting eyes directly on the head. But cover them with primer before you go on to leading your decoy.

For the larger decoys, I punch out five-sixteenths-inch (.79 cm) circles from the leftover pieces of metal I used for the fins. If you don't have a circle cutter, which is quite costly for just a few eyes, you can just as well saw them out or cut them with your shears. If they don't turn out perfectly round, shape them up with a file.

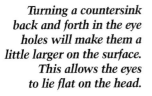

Turning a countersink back and forth in the eye holes will make them a little larger on the surface. This allows the eyes to lie flat on the head.

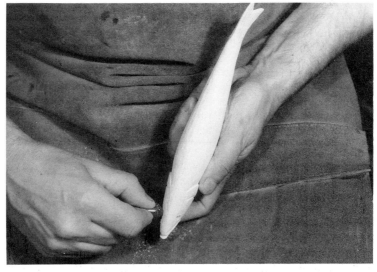

In order to attach these eyes securely, solder a piece of copper wire to the back and cut it so that it's just less than a quarter-inch (.64 cm) long. After you've painted your decoy, you'll glue the wire into an eighth-inch (.32 cm) hole drilled a quarter-inch (.64 cm) deep where you marked the eyes. You can actually drill these holes as soon as you decide you're going to make this type of eyes. I usually drill them at the same time I'm fitting the fins. And it's a good idea to make the holes a little wider on the surface by turning a countersink or three-eighths-inch (.95 cm) drill bit back and forth in the hole. This way, you'll make room for the solder, and the eyes will lie flat against the head.

To make the eyes come alive, paint a black dot in the center. But sand them lightly with steel wool or extra-fine sandpaper before you paint them to make sure they're clear of any grease or grime that will stop the paint from adhering properly. Set them aside and glue them on later with the fins.

Don't stop at the suggestions I've presented here. Search through the hobby shops and craft shops where you'll find all sorts of items that will make good fish decoy eyes. Some things I've seen used are: beads, marbles, doll eyes, plastic animal eyes, pins, screws, and even pencil erasers. So don't be afraid to improvise when it comes time to add the eyes. Use whatever satisfies your fancy.

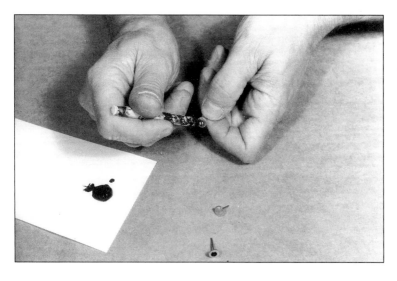

I make the eyes come alive by applying a dot of black acrylic paint with a pencil.

8

Weight and Balance

With your decoy carved, the fins cut and attached temporarily (permanently if you plan to paint them), and your line-tie in place, you're ready to begin the process of weighting and balancing your decoy. I consider this phase the most crucial of the decoy-making process, because if you don't place just the right amount of lead in just the right places, you'll have to make some very difficult adjustments to get your decoy to work properly.

Your chances of getting the weight and balance correct on the first try are very good, however, if you hollowed out as much of the belly as I recommended. If you actually made the cavity a quarter-inch (.64 cm) wide from the gill covers to the anal fin, and slightly more than halfway through the decoy, then it should be larger than needed. This will allow you to make the necessary adjustments as you go along, which I'll explain later. The part of the cavity not filled with lead can be finished off with wood filler.

Traditionally, however, most decoy carvers clear just enough space from the belly so that it can be completely filled with lead. This is sometimes a hit-and-miss proposition, unless you've done enough decoys to know just how much lead will weight each one properly and just where to place it for the correct balance. Many decoys don't turn out just right the first time, and adjustments must be made. If a decoy is too light or not balanced correctly, lead must be added somewhere to correct the problem. If it turns out to be too heavy, about the only way to remove some lead is to drill it out, and then this hole has to be filled with something else.

Most fishermen and decoy carvers are very fussy about the swimming action of their decoys, particularly the speed, and a very small amount of lead can cause a drastic change in performance. But by making the cavity in the belly larger than necessary and filling the rest with wood filler, you can more easily get the swimming action you prefer.

Although many spearmen like a fast, heavy decoy (which is necessary if they're fishing waters where there's a stiff current), I've always preferred a slow, smooth-floating decoy that can be manipulated more easily with the jigging line than a heavy decoy that basically follows the curve of its tail. But the idea that a fast decoy is better than a slow one, or vice versa, is probably more a fisherman's preference than a fish's choice. And, as any fisherman knows, your own confidence in a particular lure is often just as important as the lure itself, provided it meets the basic functional requirements.

SETTING UP

Before you begin the leading process, prepare the area where you plan to work. Set up all the equipment you'll need, see to it that you have the proper safety items, and make sure there is plenty of ventilation.

My first recommendation, as far as equipment goes, is to find yourself a hot plate or gas burner you can take outside or into the basement near an open window. If you plan to make several decoys, you should invest in an electric lead-melting pot. There are two basic types. One is just what the name implies: a small, cast-iron pot that you can dip or pour from. The other type is a raised cylindrical pot (called an electric furnace) that pours from a spout underneath. All you need to do is hold your decoy belly up under the spout, lift the handle on the side of the pot, and a small stream of lead will flow into the belly cavity. This is a safe, clean way to lead your decoy. One other lead-melting pot you may consider is the propane type that plumbers use. (Two lead-melting pots are pictured in Chapter 4.)

If you have neither a lead-melting pot nor a hot plate, the kitchen stove will suffice. Find yourself a sturdy pan made from heavy metal that will hold the heat long enough to keep the lead molten while you pour. Some pans lose their heat as soon as they're removed from the burner, which causes the lead to harden almost immediately. Perfect for the job is a small cast-iron frying pan. No matter what kind of pan you choose, however, be sure it's never used for cooking once you've melted lead in it.

The lead itself is not hard to find. I buy it by the pound in thin sheets from the scrap-metal yard. I like this form because it's easy to cut into small pieces for the lead pot. I cut it with a pair of hefty tin snips.

I've also used wheel weights that I picked up from a garage. They'll do fine once they're melted down, but they're usually greasy when you get them. If they're not clean when heated, they can produce a good deal of smoke and odor. Also, the steel clip

Lead from wheel weights and old fishing sinkers can be melted down and used to weight your decoy. But I prefer lead sheets, which are easy to cut into small pieces for the lead-melting pot.

that holds them to the wheel should be cut off. If you use one of the lead pots described above, these clips can become jammed inside the pot and cause you trouble. If you're using a pan on a hot plate, you can simply let them melt away from the lead and take them out of the pan with a pair of pliers.

Once you start pouring the lead into your decoy, you'll need a sink or tub of water close by, because you're not going to pour all the lead in at once. Plan ahead and get the water ready while the lead is melting.

It will take fifteen or twenty minutes for your lead to melt. During that time, prepare our decoy by setting the fins in place and attaching a line to the line-tie eyelet so that you can test it for proper weight and balance as you add the lead.

Be sure to protect yourself against injury from the molten lead. Wear a long-sleeved shirt and long pants, as well as a pair of gloves. Safety glasses are a must to protect your eyes from any lead that may splatter out of the lead pot. And there's a good possibility of this happening when you're working with the combination of

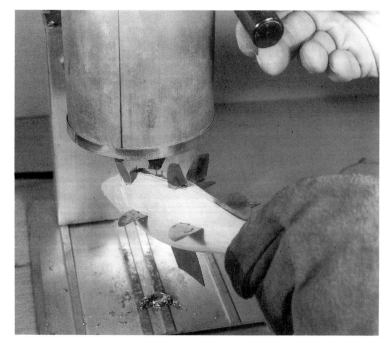

Gradually fill the belly with lead. Test the decoy in the water every so often during the weighting process to see how it balances. Be sure to pour the water out of the belly cavity before adding more lead, and wear protective clothing and safety glasses.

water and molten lead. When water gets into a pot of hot lead, it can actually cause a small explosion that will send lead flying in every direction. So be sure any lead you add to a hot lead pot is clean and dry.

FILLING THE BELLY

When all the preparations are taken care of and the lead is melted, you're ready to weight and balance your decoy. And remember, all your fins must be in place when you weight the decoy; otherwise, it won't be properly balanced.

Start by holding the decoy by the tail end. Tip it nose-down and pour just enough lead in the belly so that it runs toward the front of the cavity, but not back past the center of it. Keep this angle and dip the decoy in the tub of water you have nearby. The lead will harden almost immediately.

This probably won't be enough to sink your decoy, but turn it over on its belly anyway and check to see how close you are to the desired weight. Take it back to the lead pot (be sure to pour the water out of the belly cavity) and add more lead, always adding to the front of the cavity. If your decoy is nose-heavy, that's perfectly

A well-balanced decoy should hang nearly parallel to the bottom of the testing tub, as this one does. It should also float to the bottom in a smooth, forward motion.

okay (in fact, that's what you want unless the cavity is filled and it's still nose-heavy) because it's always easier to bring the tail down in the water than the head.

Every time you add a little more lead, bring your decoy over to the tub, submerge it—belly up—to harden the lead, then turn it over and test it. What you're trying to achieve is a decoy that sinks in the water—not like a rock, but fairly quickly—and hangs parallel to the bottom of the tub when suspended from the line-tie.

To test the decoy's swimming action, pull it up and let it float back down. Do this a number of times. If it has a metal tail, turn it so that it will make sharp turns in the confines of the tub. If it has a wooden tail, the turn will be too broad for the tub, so you won't get a really good feel for the decoy's action. But at least you'll be able to see if it floats back down in a forward motion after you pull it up. And that's what you must achieve. If your decoy doesn't swim forward, then you have a problem. But if your line-tie is in the correct spot—about a quarter of the way from the nose to the tail—and the decoy hangs parallel to the bottom of the tub, then it should swim correctly.

After leading, and when the wood is dry, fill the remaining space with wood filler. I use a putty knife for the job.

When the wood filler has hardened, carve away the excess.

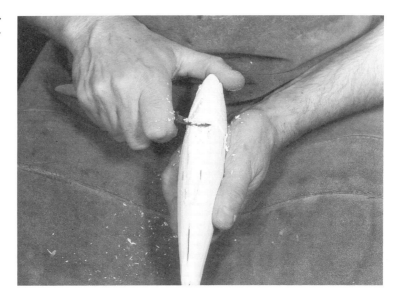

If for some reason you filled the belly cavity full with lead, and the decoy hangs either nose-down or tail-down, you can always drill excess lead out of one end of the cavity or the other to lighten it. But if you made the cavity deep enough, you should have room to spare, especially toward the tail, where you can add a bit more lead if the tail floats too high.

When you're satisfied with the swimming action of your decoy, set it aside and let it dry thoroughly, preferably overnight. Next day, when the wood is no longer wet, fill the rest of the cavity with a waterproof wood filler (actually overfill it to allow for shrinkage). The brands of filler-sealant that I use are white Famowood or DAP Wood Dough, but Plastic Wood cellulose fiber filler will also do. If you use something else, be sure you know it will not break down under prolonged exposure to water.

Let the wood filler set overnight, or until you know it's totally dry. You can then test your decoy one more time in the water to see that it still swims the way it did before you added the wood filler. If it doesn't, make the necessary adjustments now, before you paint it.

If you're not going to paint the fins, and they're attached only temporarily, pull them off now and dry your decoy with a cloth or

After carving the excess wood filler away, sand it smooth with a piece of medium grit sandpaper.

towel. Carve away the excess wood filler and sand the belly smooth. Cover it with your sealer and primer and let it dry. You may even want to give the whole body another coat of primer. When the sealer and primer are completely dry, you're ready to paint your decoy.

Color Guide with Painting and Carving Notes

This is a reference and guide for painting the decoys that can be carved from the patterns in Chapter 5. I have also included special notes on carving that you'll find helpful when dealing with the subtle variations of detail from species to species.

There are two sections: one on the larger decoys (which are more detailed and truer to the fish species they depict) and another on the smaller ones (which are less detailed and, in some cases, completely nonrepresentational in their coloration).

The basic painting procedures that can generally be applied to both large and small decoys painted in a realistic style are explained in Chapter 9.

The painting information accompanying each of the photos in this section describes how to make mixtures that approximate the colors depicted. It's not necessary to achieve these exact colors. Instead, mix your paints until the colors satisfy your taste, because you must keep in mind that you're painting a decoy to lure fish, and just about every color and color combination imaginable have been known to do that. If you want to duplicate an actual living species, consult the fish books listed in the bibliography.

Rainbow Trout

PAINTING NOTES

Belly: Titanium White.
Sides: Titanium White. Paint each side to about eye level.
Back: Two parts French Ultramarine Blue mixed with one part Cadmium Orange. Add a touch of Lamp Black and darken to your satisfaction.
Markings: Paint a narrow strip of Cadmium Deep Red on each side over the Titanium White and brush it out to create a slash of pink. Dot the entire fish with small random black dots.

CARVING NOTES

The rainbow trout has a slightly forked tail, and the upper jaw does not extend past the eye.

FINS

The fins are copper.

Brown Trout

PAINTING NOTES

Belly: Titanium White. Paint the belly only up to the pectoral and pelvic fin slots.

Sides: Yellow Ochre. Paint the sides to the top of the gill covers.

Back: Five parts Raw Umber mixed with one part French Ultramarine Blue and one part Cadmium Orange. Add a touch of Lamp Black and darken to your satisfaction.

Markings: Paint several dots of Titanium White on each side and add a smaller dot of Lamp Black in the center of each white dot to create a halo effect. Paint several dots with French Ultramarine Blue (lightened with a touch of Titanium White) on each side, adding a smaller dot of Cadmium Deep Red in the center. Finally, dot the entire fish with small random black dots.

CARVING NOTES

The upper jaw on the brown trout extends past the eye.

FINS

The fins and tail are copper.

Brook Trout

PAINTING NOTES

Belly: Titanium White. Paint with the belly color only up to the pectoral and pelvic fin slots.

Lower sides: One part Cadmium Deep Red mixed with one part Cadmium Yellow Light. A Lamp Black line separates the lower side color from the white belly.

Upper sides: One part French Ultramarine Blue mixed with one part Cadmium Yellow Light. Paint with this color to the top of the gill covers.

Back: Take a portion of the upper-side color and darken it with a small amount of Lamp Black.

Markings: Paint small wormlike squiggles, or vermiculations, on the back from the head to the tail with Cadmium Yellow Light. With the same color, paint small random dots on each side. Paint several dots with French Ultramarine Blue (lightened with a touch of Titanium White) on each side, adding a smaller dot of Cadmium Deep Red in the center. Paint the tail with the light green used on the sides and add two or three dark green irregular lines across the tail.

CARVING NOTES

The upper jaw on the brook trout extends past the eye, and the tail is cut straight across. This is why the brook trout is called squaretail in some regions of the country.

FINS

The fins are brass.

Lake Trout

PAINTING NOTES

Belly: Titanium White. Paint the belly up to the pectoral and pelvic fin slots.

Sides: Four parts Titanium White mixed with one to two parts Lamp Black and two to three parts Raw Umber. Paint to the top of the gill covers with this color.

Back: Take a portion of the side color and darken it to your satisfaction with a small bit of Lamp Black and Raw Umber.

Markings: Paint the sides and tail with various-sized dots of Titanium White. (If you want to tone these dots down a bit, add a very small amount of Lamp Black to the Titanium White.)

CARVING NOTES

The lake trout has a strongly forked tail, and the upper jaw extends past the eye.

FINS

The fins are copper.

Perch

PAINTING NOTES

Belly: Titanium White. Paint the belly up to the pectoral fin slots.

Sides: Cadmium Yellow Light. Paint each side to about eye level.

Back: Two parts French Ultramarine Blue mixed with one part Cadmium Orange. Add a small amount of Lamp Black and Raw Umber and darken to your satisfaction.

Markings: With the back color, mark five or six bars opposite one another on each side. Shape them so that they come to a narrow peak just below the side fin slots. Blend them into the back by lightly brushing and dabbing along the line where the back and side colors meet. Paint the pectoral fins with Cadmium Orange mixed with a very small portion of Cadmium Yellow Light; this gives your decoy a touch of that orange-yellow one usually associates with the perch. Lighten the color of the tail by painting it first with Cadmium Yellow Light and then with the back color.

CARVING NOTES

For variety and added color, the pectoral fins are burned in and painted.

FINS

The fins are brass.

Smallmouth Bass

PAINTING NOTES

Belly: Titanium White. Paint up to the mouth level.

Sides: One part Cadmium Orange mixed with one part French Ultramarine Blue. Paint to the top of the gill cover.

Back: Add a small amount of Lamp Black to a portion of the side color. Darken it enough to suit yourself, knowing that some smallmouth bass are extremely dark.

Markings: With the back color, paint several bars of varying length on each side; blend them into the back. Paint the lines on each side of the head from the eye to the edge of the gill cover; use the back color. Paint a small white spot on the tip of the gill covers and a black spot next to it.

CARVING NOTES

The upper jaw on the smallmouth bass does not extend beyond the eye.

FINS

The fins are brass.

Largemouth Bass

PAINTING NOTES

Belly: Titanium White. Paint the belly and continue with this color halfway up both sides.

Back: One part French Ultramarine Blue mixed with one part Cadmium Orange. Add a bit of Cadmium Yellow Light if you prefer to brighten the green hue. Add just a touch of Lamp Black if you want a darker shade.

Sides: Bring the back color down to the white sides and blend it into the belly paint.

Markings: Using the back color, mark off several spots opposite one another on each side along a centerline. Make them wider by dabbing with a small brush. Paint the lines on each side of the head from the eye to the edge of the gill cover; use the back color. The gill covers can be finished with a small spot of white on the tip and a black spot next to it.

CARVING NOTES

The upper jaw on the largemouth bass extends well beyond the eye.

FINS

The fins are brass.

Sucker

PAINTING NOTES

Belly: Titanium White. Paint up to the pectoral and pelvic fins.
Sides: Cadmium Yellow Light. Paint to eye level.
Back: Five parts Raw Umber mixed with one part Lamp Black.
Markings: Mix one part Cadmium Deep Red with one part Cadmium Yellow Light for the pectoral fins, pelvic fins, and tail.

CARVING NOTES

The mouth on the sucker is carved rather than cut out as it is on the other decoys. You can do this by turning a countersink (or a drill bit) by hand under the snout, creating a shallow hole. Draw a circle around this hole about an eighth of an inch (.32 cm) away from it. Make a cut along this line with the tip of your knife, then trim the wood away from around it. This creates a suckerlike mouth that protrudes slightly from the body. The pectoral and pelvic fins are burned in and painted.

FINS

The fins are brass.

Pike

PAINTING NOTES

Belly: Titanium White. Paint up to the pectoral and pelvic fin slots.
Sides: Two parts Cadmium Yellow Light mixed with one part French Ultramarine Blue. Paint each side to the top of the gill covers.
Back: Take a portion of the side color and create a dark green by adding a small amount of Lamp Black or Raw Umber.
Markings: Paint several small, bean-shaped spots on each side (including the gill covers) with Titanium White. Paint several small black dots on the tail.

FINS

The fins are brass.

Tiger Musky

PAINTING NOTES

Belly: Titanium White. Paint up to the pectoral and pelvic fin slots.

Sides: Titanium White mixed with just a slight touch of French Ultramarine Blue. Paint the sides to eye level.

Back: Raw Umber mixed with a touch of Burnt Sienna (or Cadmium Orange).

Markings: With the back color, paint several irregularly shaped bars on each side. Dry-brush them so that they subtly blend into the side color.

FINS

The fins and tail are copper.

Great Lakes Musky

PAINTING NOTES

Belly: Titanium White. Paint up to the pectoral and pelvic fin slots.

Sides: Three parts Titanium White mixed with one part Lamp Black (or enough to suit your taste). Paint each side to eye level.

Back: Use a portion of the side color and mix in an additional amount of Lamp Black until it is dark gray or charcoal black.

Markings: Paint black dots of varying sizes in random order on each side, including the tail.

FINS

The fins are copper.

Sunfish

PAINTING NOTES

Belly: One part Cadmium Deep Red mixed with one part Cadmium Orange. Paint nearly to eye level and back to the end of the anal fin slot.
Sides: Cadmium Yellow Light undercoat. Paint over with the back color.
Back: Two parts French Ultramarine Blue mixed with one part Cadmium Yellow Light and a touch of Cadmium Orange. Paint both the back and the sides (over the yellow undercoat) with the back color. Blend with the belly color.
Markings: With the back color, paint four or five bars opposite one another on each side. Mottle the sides between the bars with Cadmium Yellow Light. Add just a touch of Titanium White and Cadmium Yellow Light to a sizable dab of French Ultramarine Blue and paint lines on each side of the head. Paint a narrow line on the tip of each gill cover with Cadmium Deep Red and a slightly wider black line in front of it.

CARVING NOTES

The upper jaw is rounded at the ends and is carved all the way around the top of the snout.

FINS

The fins and tail are copper.

Walleye

PAINTING NOTES

Belly: Titanium White. Paint the belly up to the pectoral fin slots.
Sides: Yellow Ochre. Paint each side to just above the eye.
Back: Two parts French Ultramarine Blue mixed with one part Cadmium Orange. Add a small amount of Lamp Black and Raw Umber and darken it to your satisfaction.
Markings: With the back color, mark five to seven bars opposite one another on each side. Shape them so that they are somewhat irregular and narrower at the bottom, stopping about midway down the side. Blend them into the back by lightly brushing and dabbing along the line where the back and side colors meet. Mottle the sides very lightly with the back color. Lighten the color of the tail by first painting it with Yellow Ochre and then with the back color; lightly draw two or three narrow lines running across the tail on each side.

FINS

The fins are brass.

Small Trout

These three trout are carved from the small trout pattern. They are painted in a similar manner to the larger examples of each species. The fins and tail on the brook trout are brass; the others have copper fins.

Small Perch

The color mixes and painting procedures are the same for this small perch as they are for the large one. The fins and tail are copper.

Small Bass

These two small bass are painted similarly to their larger counterparts, but with less detail. The smallmouth on the left has copper fins and tail; those on the largemouth are brass.

Small Sucker

Follow the painting instructions accompanying the larger sucker. Attach the floating fins by punching a hole in the center and screwing them into the belly, as pictured in Chapter 7. The mouth is carved in the same manner as described for the larger sucker. The fins are brass.

Small Musky and Pike

The painting instructions for these two decoys accompany the larger Great Lakes Musky and Pike. Note the two line-tie eyelets on the pike. The fins and tail on the musky are copper; those on the pike are brass.

Frog and Mouse

Pike and muskies are interested not only in fish, but in other creatures as well. The metal on both the frog and the mouse decoys is brass. The hind legs on the frog are soldered together, and the foot is bent up at a ninety-degree angle to act as a rudder so that the decoy will circle in the water. The mouse has small map tacks for eyes, and rubber skirting material used on fishing lures serves as whiskers.

When I paint frogs and mice, I never stick to one pattern or color combination. I see them as whimsical critters and play with different paints, colors, and finishes.

Small Sunfish

These two sunfish decoys are painted in a fanciful style with acrylic paint. The brilliance of their colors is brought out with a coat of clear lacquer, which is also a protective finish. Red and white decoys have always been popular with pike fishermen, but many other imaginative color combinations and patterns are used, too. The metal on the red and yellow decoy is copper; the red and white one has brass fins.

9

Painting

There are many attitudes and approaches to painting fish decoys depending upon your desired end product. They can range anywhere from extremely detailed, realistic painting to simple one-color stain rubbed onto the raw wood and covered with a coat of varnish. In fact, the most common color pattern for fish decoys could well be the simple two-tone red and white combination, usually with a red head and a white body.

NONREPRESENTATIONAL PAINTING

If you keep in mind that fish decoys are made to attract fish, just as a plug or Dardevle lure is, then you know that they don't necessarily have to be painted to represent anything living. Many times, the brightest and most bizarre-looking lures are the most effective. And you can probably find as many fish decoys with dots, stripes, and other abstract designs as with realistic color schemes.

The paints decoy makers have used down through the years are just as varied as the color schemes. So don't feel that you have to rush out and stock up on a whole line of paints, brushes, thinners, lacquers, and varnishes. Because you don't, especially if you paint your decoy in a nonrepresentational style of your own.

If you do paint your decoy in this way, consider using paint you already have around the house. And if it's not an exterior grade that will hold up in the water, cover it with lacquer or exterior varnish when it's dry.

Paints and other coloring media you might consider using are artists' oils and acrylics, latex and oil-based house paints, model paints, auto paints, fingernail polish (some wild colors are available), wood stains, food coloring, and even shoe polish. You don't have to be particular as to how you apply them, either. Fish-decoy makers paint with rags, sponges, sticks, palette knives, brushes, spray cans, air brushes, and even their fingers.

If you're wondering about your painting skills, don't worry. Paint your decoy however you like. Let your imagination run wild and enjoy it. If you don't like it the first time, paint it again; an extra coat of paint will add more protection for the wood.

REPRESENTATIONAL PAINTING

There is also a long tradition of realistically painted fish decoys. It's not so much an attempt to paint an exact copy of a specific fish, frog, or other creature, but more of an attempt to be close enough to make the decoy identifiable, leaving plenty of room for personal interpretation. And that's the joy of painting fish decoys: you don't have to worry whether your colors are perfectly mixed, or your markings are just so. Furthermore, as any fisherman knows, individual fish within a species can show quite a bit of variation from one another in color and markings.

I usually paint my decoys in this tradition and will explain the process for you here. Considering that there is so much freedom in the degree of realism you need to achieve, you'll find it's not as difficult or tedious as you might imagine.

Paints and supplies. I recommend you cover the raw wood with a sealer, a primer, or both, as explained in Chapter 6, before you weight and balance your decoy. But if you didn't, do it now and let it dry. I usually just gesso my decoys rather than apply a sealer first. But it's arguably better to first seal and then prime the wood for painting.

As far as paints go, I prefer to use either regular artists' oils or artists' alkyd oils. There are a couple of reasons for this. First of all, these paints hold up extremely well on decoys that are repeatedly immersed in water, and you don't really have to protect them with varnish or lacquer, either. Secondly, fish painting requires considerable blending, and the fact that these paints don't begin to dry for hours after you mix them makes them ideal for this.

Most bird and duck-decoy carvers use acrylic paints, primarily for carvings that won't be used in the water. You may want to paint your fish decoys with acrylics too. But unless you use many thin washes, you'll probably find blending difficult. And you should give these paints a waterproof protective finish when they dry.

The regular artists' oils and the alkyd oil paints are comparably priced and are sold at art-supply stores. Their permanency ratings are equal and they feel almost identical when you mix them and paint with them. You can usually get them in the same colors, and they can both be thinned with turpentine or paint thinner. There is one major difference between the two, however. The alkyds dry much faster—usually within forty-eight hours—whereas the regular artists' oils can take up to a week or more to dry.

There are a couple of tricks that you can use to get the regular oils to dry faster. If you mix them half-and-half with the alkyds, they'll dry just about as fast as the alkyds alone. There are also a number of drying agents you can buy to speed up the drying time of the artists' oils. Some of them are difficult to manage, however, so you'll have to experiment a little until you understand them well. I personally use the Liquin-brand oil painting medium. And I find that when regular oil paints are mixed with an equal amount of this medium, they'll dry just about as quickly as the alkyds.

As far as knowing which colors to buy, you don't have to go out and buy every individual color you think you'll use. With a few basic paints, you can mix every color necessary for freshwater fish. At the very most, you'll need the following colors: *Titanium White, Lamp Black, Burnt Umber, Cadmium Deep Red, French Ultramarine Blue, Yellow Ochre, Cadmium Yellow Light,* and *Cadmium Orange.* Study the color descriptions presented with the color plates and buy only the colors necessary to paint your particular decoy. A color wheel, available at art-supply stores, will help you mix these and other colors you may want to try.

Use paint thinner or turpentine, preferably the odorless type, to thin these paints. Be sure to have plenty of ventilation in the room, but if you don't, and you paint for a long period of time, wear a chemical mask.

Brushes, you'll discover, involve a matter of personal preference. Once you've done a lot of painting, you'll get used to certain shapes, sizes, and hair textures and will learn exactly which ones are right for you.

I personally like good, soft, natural-bristle brushes for the belly, and soft synthetic brushes for the rest of the body. I find the popular sable brushes much *too* soft for my style of blending and they don't last very long painting on wood the way I do, either.

If you're just starting out as a painter, you can get off to a good start with only three or four brushes. A quarter-inch (.64 cm) and three-eighths-inch (.95 cm) flat and a number 2 or number 3 round are good choices to start with. Natural-bristle brushes are fine if you're not familiar with the many different types of hair. You can learn which brushes are right for you by talking to the people who work in the art-supply stores. Most of them are artists

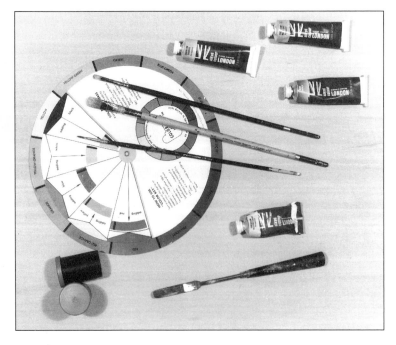

Some recommended painting supplies include brushes, tubes of alkyd oil paints, a palette knife, a color wheel, and two 35mm film cans for storing leftover paint in the freezer.

Mix all the colors you'll need for your decoy before you start to paint. Here I mix my colors on a pad of disposable paper palette sheets.

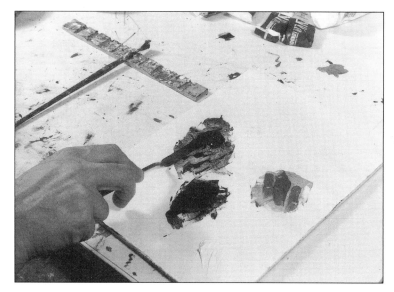

themselves and are quite familiar with the supplies they're selling. Now and then buy a new brush that looks and feels like something you could use. This way you'll soon learn what you like and will build up an assortment of brushes.

You'll also need some sort of palette and palette knife for mixing your paints. A piece of glass or white plastic works fine as a palette, but tablets of palette sheets are available that you can simply tear out and throw away when you clean up each day.

Get yourself a few rags, an old shirt or apron, a couple of small cans for some thinner, and you're ready to paint.

An easy method. Specific color mixes and painting instructions appear along with the individual decoys in the color section. You don't have to stick to these exactly, but you may save yourself some time, paint, and frustration if you do—at least until you get a feel for it. As mentioned earlier, a color wheel, or key, will also help. And remember, you won't need a whole lot of paint for each decoy; a dab of each color no larger than a quarter will probably be sufficient.

If you're new at painting, don't start right in on your decoy. Cover a piece of wood with gesso and practice on that first. This way, you'll get a feel for your paints and brushes and will also have a test sample for protective finishes when your paint is dry.

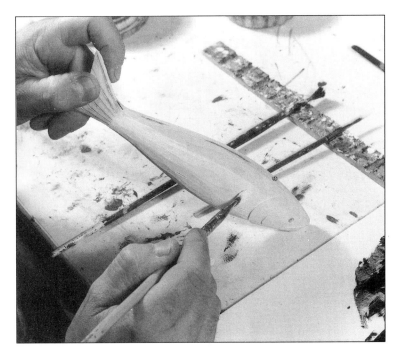

When painting the rainbow trout, as pictured here, bring the white belly-color up to just above the eyes. Hold your decoy by the tail and rest the lower jaw on the table while you paint.

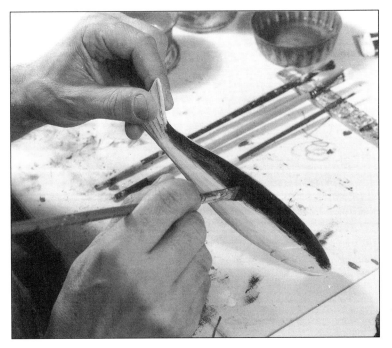

Paint the back and blend it into the side color.

If you're painting a decoy with a metal or leather tail, wedge a piece of scrap metal in the tail-slot and use that as a handle to hold your decoy while you paint. Otherwise, hold it by the wooden tail.

Mix your alkyd paints on the palette with your palette knife, adding a slight amount of thinner or turpentine as you mix. Use a clean brush to transfer the thinning medium onto the palette, but thin these paints only slightly relative to their consistency as it is when they come directly from the tube; you don't want them to be so thin that they're watery.

A good place to begin painting your decoy is the inside of the mouth, which I usually paint white. Paint the belly next and bring this color up to the sides for varying distances depending on the species of fish.

Paint the sides next, blending this color into the belly by brushing it down and bringing the belly color up. Be sure to wipe your

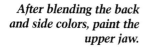

After blending the back and side colors, paint the upper jaw.

brush dry before blending so that you'll be nearly dry-brushing the two colors together. That gives you good control of the blending process.

Paint the back next and bring this color down to meet the side color. Blend the side and back paints together in the same manner as explained above for blending the side and belly colors.

With most fish, I like to darken the cheeks by bringing the back color down a little farther on the head. But that's a personal preference you may prefer not to adopt. Finish the head by painting the upper jaw with the back color.

The next step is painting the detail. With some fish, the detail markings amount to nothing more than dots of one color. With others, you get into dots of varying colors and sizes, dots within dots, bars, and stripes that require additional blending. I have therefore included the explanation for painting the detail on each individual species along with the other information accompanying the color photos.

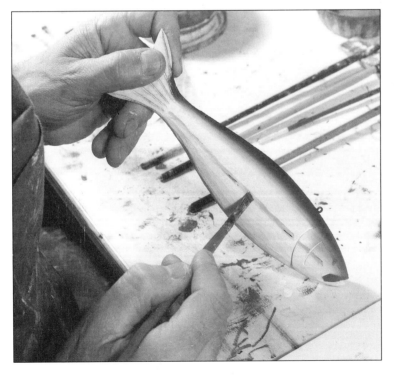

To get the pink slash on the sides of the rainbow trout, paint a narrow strip of Cadmium Deep Red over the white. Spread and blend it with a dry brush.

The rainbow trout is covered with dots on the sides and back. To make each side approximately the same, count the dots as you paint them on.

Paint the tail by resting the snout on the table while you hold the decoy in this manner.

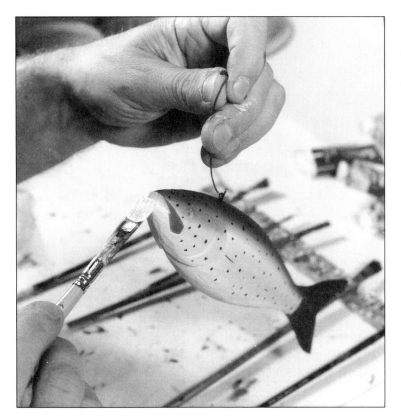

Touch up the snout and tips of the tail while you hold the decoy by a wire hooked through the line-tie eyelet. Hang the decoy to dry with this wire also.

If your decoy has a wooden tail, that will be the last thing to paint. You may find the best time to paint it is a day or two after you've painted the body, when the paint has dried. But if you want to finish the complete paint job in one work period, hold the decoy with the top and bottom tips of the tail between your thumb and index finger (rest the snout on the table) and paint it on both sides with the back color (or a combination of the back and side color to give it a brighter, somewhat translucent look) and add the necessary detail markings.

Finally, hold the decoy by a wire hooked through the screw-eye and touch up the finger marks left on the tail where you held it. Also check the lower jaw and nose to see whether they need any touching up. Look over the rest of the body to make sure there is nothing else you missed. If there is nothing else, hang the decoy to dry for at least forty-eight hours, and when there is no danger of smearing the paint, put your decoy together and test it in the water.

Be sure to clean your brushes thoroughly with paint thinner or turpentine when you've finished painting. If you do, they'll last a long time. And if you have a good bit of paint left over, oils will keep for weeks in the freezer if stored in small plastic film cans.

10

Putting It All Together

Now that your decoy is carved, weighted, and painted, you're almost finished. The only thing you really have left to do is to attach the fins and eyes. While the paint is drying (let it sit at least forty-eight hours, to be on the safe side), turn your attention to the jigging stick.

JIGGING STICK

The jigging stick is an essential part of both the craft of fish-decoy making and the sport of ice fishing, because it's the connection between the fisherman in the shanty and his decoy below. In fact, many carvers and fishermen get so used to the feel of a certain type that without it they lose confidence in their ability to work the decoy properly. So the jigging stick, for many, is an extension of the fish decoy itself.

There are two basic styles of jigging sticks, each of which to some degree represents regional preferences. The first one — commonly used in Wisconsin, especially among the Ojibway Indians — is the "stick" style. To make this type of jigging stick, use a small twig or branch a half-inch (1.3 cm) to an inch (2.5 cm) in diameter and about a foot (30.5 cm) long (the length can vary according to feel). Skin the bark off (unless you like the feel of it as it is) and sand the stick smooth. The ends need to be rounded so that there are no sharp edges to fray the line you'll wrap around it later. You can do this with your knife, rasp, or a piece of sandpaper.

Now, an inch or so from the end, cut a notch for the line. It should be no more than an eighth of an inch (.32 cm) deep and an inch or inch-and-a-half (2.5 cm or 3.8 cm) long all the way around the stick. Smooth it off with a piece of sandpaper, and you've got yourself a jigging stick.

Tie about ten yards of twenty- or thirty-pound-test (9 kg or 14 kg) fishing line to the notched section and wrap it on. Many fishermen still prefer cloth line to monofilament because it's easier to see in the dimness of the shanty and has less of a tendency to twist and tangle. But if you think the invisibility of monofilament is less apt to spook a leery fish, go ahead and use it.

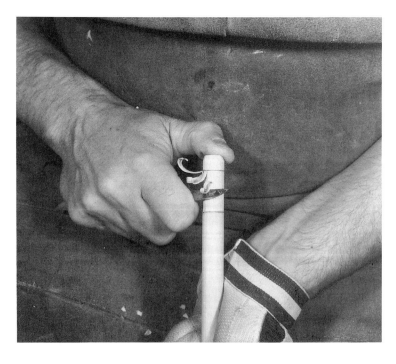

A jigging stick can be made by cutting a notch in a half-inch (1.3 cm) dowel. Be sure to sand the carved area and round the ends so they won't fray the line.

Remember, your decoy will be swimming in a circular motion all day long, which will cause your line to twist unless you attach a swivel to it. The common thing to do is to tie a snap swivel to the end of the jigging line. This not only prevents the line from twisting but also allows you to move the line from hole to hole on a multiple line-tie and to change decoys more easily.

This stick-type jigging stick can also be made in the same way from a three-eighths- to one-inch-diameter (.95 cm to 2.5 cm) dowel. Or you can carve one of your own design from a piece of good-looking hardwood, adding intricately carved designs in much the same way European folk artists embellish many of their hand-made utilitarian items.

The second type of jigging stick is the V-notched stick. It is made less for a specific feel of jigging than for ease of wrapping and unwrapping the line without tangles. Although a fisherman who uses this kind of stick may hold it directly in his hand the whole time he's working his decoy, he most likely will simply let the desired amount of line out and attach the stick to the wall or ceiling above the hole, working the decoy by holding the line. I actually prefer fishing this way, because it allows me to have both hands free for spearing. I can also hang a second decoy in the water and work it alternately or simultaneously with the first.

To make this type of jigging stick, use a small piece of wood a quarter- to a half-inch (.64 to 1.3 cm) thick, two or three inches (5.1 or 7.6 cm) wide, and about six inches (15 cm) long. Cut a

Three jigging sticks with line and snap swivels. The top one is made from a half-inch (1.3 cm) dowel, the one in the center is carved from a twig, and the bottom one is the typical V-notched type with an extra snap swivel attached to it.

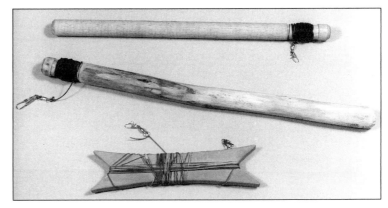

V-shaped notch a half-inch (1.3 cm) deep in each end and sand it smooth. Wrap your fishing line on it both length-wise and around it. Attach a snap swivel to the line and you're ready to go.

PROTECTIVE FINISHES

When the paint on your decoy has finally dried thoroughly, you can get back to it and finish up. If you painted the fins along with the body, your job is complete and the decoy is ready to use. But there is a decision you'll have to make at this point: whether or not to cover your paint with a protective finish.

My feeling in this matter is to leave the paint as it is, because fish decoys become scratched, marred, and battered even under the most careful use, so they need to be repaired and repainted now and again. If the paint is left bare, you can easily touch up or repaint your decoy at any time directly over the old paint. If you cover it with a protective coating, however, repainting won't be so simple. You'll probably have to lay down a primer first or paint it with more than one coat.

Still, there are advantages to covering your paint with a protective finish. A good hard finish, such as lacquer or varnish, will protect against minor scratches and scuffing and give your wood added protection against the water. If you use a high-gloss finish, it will also add shine and luster to your colors and may increase their attractiveness to the fish.

If you do decide to use a protective finish, test it to see that it's compatible with your paint before you apply it to your decoy. Try it out on the piece of wood you practiced painting on before you actually painted your decoy. This way, you'll also find out whether the paint is completely dry. And it's actually better to spray, rather than brush, the finish on. Sometimes repeated brushing will wear off paint that wouldn't be affected by spraying.

Be sure also that the finish you choose won't be affected by prolonged exposure to water and won't drastically alter the colors of your paints. Most exterior varnishes, though they may be great protective finishes, have a yellowish tint that tends to muddy the color of your paints as soon as you apply them. And this effect increases over time.

There are some good plastic finishes that go on clear and remain that way for years, but I actually recommend clear, high-gloss lacquer. It's perfectly clear when you first apply it and remains that way after many coats. With only one coat it won't be extremely glossy, but each additional application increases the shine as well as the intensity of your colors. And three or four coats will give you all the protection you'll need.

PATINAS

When I make brass or copper fins, tail, and eyes, I usually like to modify the new-metal gleam. I know that many fishermen believe that the flashier the decoy, the better, but I personally like a more subtle look. This is easy enough to achieve by using a patina solution.

Liver of sulphur, which simply darkens copper and gives brass a tarnished look, is what I generally use. It's available in both a liquid and a powder form. If you buy it as a liquid, you won't have to bother mixing a solution and will get more predictable results.

The best time to dip the fins and eyes in the solution is just before you permanently attach them to the decoy. And if you plan to solder any parts, you must do it before dipping the metal. Otherwise, the solder won't adhere to it. Also, be sure the painted

I like to soak the brass and copper fins in a liver of sulphur solution. This tarnishes these metals and gives them a subtle appearance that is appropriate for my style of decoys.

dot on the eyes is thoroughly dry so that it won't dissolve in the solution. I recommend that you wear a pair of rubber gloves to keep the chemical off your skin. And if you work outside, you can avoid filling your house with the strong rotten-egg odor of liver of sulphur.

Find yourself a shallow pan, such as an old pie tin, and pour in a cup of warm — but not hot — water. Add three or four drops of liver of sulphur with an eye dropper. Thoroughly mix the solution and the water together. Use a scrap piece of metal to test the strength of your mixture. If you've added too much liver of sulphur, your metal will turn black very quickly and you'll have to dilute it with more water. If you didn't add enough, the metal won't change color, and you'll need to add a few more drops of the solution.

When you're satisfied with the mixture, place your metal decoy parts in it and gently move them around. When they turn the color you like, take them out and place them on a towel or cloth. Wipe each piece dry as quickly as possible to keep the color uniform.

There are many other solutions available at jewelry-supply houses that will give you all kinds of patinas on brass and copper,

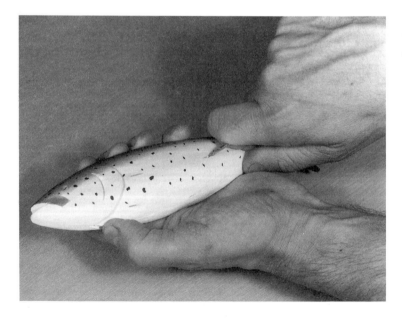

When the paint is thoroughly dry, clear the fin slots of excess paint with your knife.

and you may enjoy experimenting with some of them to see what kind of effect you can create on the fins.

ATTACHING FINS AND EYES

Once you've finished putting a patina on the fins, tail, and eyes, you can attach them to the body. But if you want to give your decoy a protective finish, you might as well give it at least one coat before you attach the hardware. With additional coats, you can also cover the fins.

If you set the side fins up with screws, fasten them now. If you're glueing the fins in place, you'll have to clear their slots of paint first. Do this by simply running your knife through the slots as you did when you cut them.

The glue I prefer for fastening the fins is a urethane glue. It's impervious to water, makes a tight bond, and doesn't harden too quickly. This allows me to work at my own pace. A waterproof epoxy, especially the slow-drying type, is also a good glue; the fast-drying type might set before you're ready and give you problems. Contact cement will also do the job, but it's a little messy and difficult to work with.

Use a thin blade to stuff glue in the fin slots, but be careful not to overfill. Insert the fins and wipe away excess glue with a cloth or paper towel.

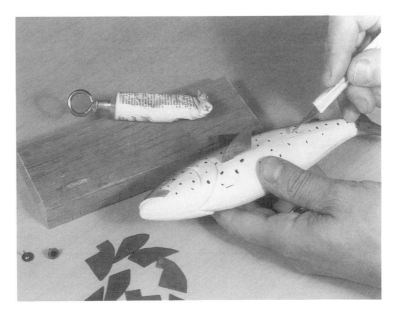

Once the fin slots are cleared, use a thin-bladed knife or single-edged razor blade to stuff glue into them. Don't overfill the slots, however, especially when using urethane glue, because it has a tendency to bubble up while setting. If you use too much, it will foam out and make cleanup tough. Wipe the excess glue from around each slot with a paper towel or cloth that you have slightly moistened with rubbing alcohol. Be careful not to rub too hard, because you don't want to take off the paint.

Now insert the fins. If they force glue out of the slots as you push them in, either wipe around them or pull them out and clear away the glue.

After you've set all the fins in place, glue in the eyes. Be sure to snip the wire pins off the backs of them to about a quarter-inch (.64 cm) so that they'll fit the holes you drilled for them. Dip the wires in the glue and cover the ends with a substantial dab. Insert them into the decoy and line the eyes up with each other. Let the glue set for twelve to twenty-four hours. When it's hard, give your decoy the final protective coats (if you've decided to cover the paint).

Snip the wire on each eye to a quarter inch (.64 cm), put a dab of glue on them, and insert them in the eye holes. Look at your decoy from different angles and line the two eyes up with each other.

I give my decoy a final test in an aquarium filled with water. It swims forward in a smooth, steady motion and hangs parallel to the bottom of the tank.

Your decoy is now complete and ready to take to the shanty or put on display. But you may want to give it one last test, and you can do that in a bathtub filled with cold water.

TESTING YOUR DECOY

Attach your jigging line to the line-tie eyelet and work the decoy up and down in the water until you get the feel of it. Bend the side fins and the tail so that you can see what effect they have on the swimming action. The way the decoy acts in the bathtub is essentially the way it will act under the ice, unless you'll be fishing in a strong current.

Even if you aren't a fisherman and don't plan on using your decoy to attract pike or muskies, you can certainly enjoy it as a bit of genuine Americana that you've created yourself. And you'll have a better understanding and appreciation of the sport of ice fishing and the craft of fish-decoy carving, both past and present.

Sources of Supplies

Carving tools and materials

Albert Constantine and Sons, Inc.
2050 Eastchester Road
Bronx, NY 10461-2297
1-800-223-8087

Al's Decoy Supplies
27 Connaught Avenue
London, Ontario
N5Y 3A4
CANADA
1-519-451-4729

Bob Morgan Woodworking Supplies
1123 Bardstown Road
Louisville, KY 40204
1-502-456-2545

Craft Woods
10921 York Road
Cockeysville, MD 21030
1-301-667-9663

Exotic Woods, Inc.
2483 Industrial Street
Burlington, Ontario
L7P 1A6
CANADA
1-416-335-8066

Leichtung Workshops
4944 Commerce Parkway
Cleveland, OH 44128
1-800-321-6840

P.C. English Enterprises, Inc.
P.O. Box 380
Thornburg, VA 22565
1-800-221-9474

Silvo Hardware Company
611 North Broadway
P.O. Box 92069
Milwaukee, WI 53202
1-800-331-1261

The Fine Tool Shops
170 West Road
P.O. Box 7091
Portsmouth, NH 03801
1-800-533-5305

The Woodworkers' Store
21801 Industrial Boulevard
Rogers, MN 55374-9514
1-612-428-2199

Tool Bin
10575 Clark Road
Davisburg, MI 48019
1-313-625-0390

Troy Woodcraft
301 Scottsdale Drive
Troy, MI 48084
1-313-689-1997

Wood Carvers Store and School
3056 Excelsior Boulevard
Minneapolis, MN 55416
1-612-927-7491

Wood Carvers Supply, Inc.
P.O. Box 8928
Norfolk, VA 23503
1-800-824-6229

Woodcraft
210 Wood County Industrial Park
P.O. Box 1686
Parkersburg, WV 26102
1-800-225-1153

Woodworker's Supply of New Mexico
5604 Alameda Place, N.E.
Albuquerque, NM 87113
1-800-645-9292

Woodworkers Warehouse
309-H Howard Avenue
Rockville, MD 20850
1-301-340-7377

Painting supplies

Chasselle, Inc.
9645 Gerwig Lane
Columbia, MD 21046
1-800-628-8608

Dick Blick
P.O. Box 1267
Galesburg, IL 61401
1-800-447-8192

Koenig Artist Supplies, Inc.
1777 Boston Post Road
Milford, CT 06460
1-800-243-4012

Wildlife Artists Supply Company
P.O. Box 967
Monroe, GA 30655
1-800-334-8012

Metalworking tools and materials

Allcraft Tool and Supply Company, Inc.
100 Frank Road
Hicksville, NY 11801
1-800-645-7124

Chaselle, Inc.
9645 Gerwig Lane
Columbia, MD 21046
1-800-628-8608

Fishing tackle supplies

Cabela's
812-13th Avenue
Sidney, NE 69160
1-800-237-4444

The Netcraft Company
2800 Tremainsville Road
Toledo, OH 43613
1-800-638-2723

Taxidermy supplies (glass eyes)

J. W. Elwood Supply Company, Inc.
Box 3507
Omaha, NE 68103
1-800-228-2291

Penn Taxidermy Supply Company
P.O. Box 156
Hazleton, PA 18201-0156
1-717-455-2431

Tohickon Glass Eyes
P.O. Box 15
Erwinna, PA 18920
1-800-441-5983

Van Dyke's
P.O. Box 278
Woonsocket, SD 57585
1-800-843-3320

Ice fishing literature

Highwood Bookshop
P.O. Box 1246
Travers City, MI 49685
1-616-271-3898
(Bibliography available: *Ice Spearing Decoys and Related Paraphernalia* by Gary L. Miller, 1987.)

The Hunting Rig
453 Pendleton Road
Neenah, WI 54596
1-414-725-4350

Fish decoy carving kits

Michigan Decoys
2416 Evans Drive
Silver Spring, MD 20902
1-301-681-9187

Collecting clubs

Great Lakes Fish Decoy Collectors and
  Carvers Association
Frank Barow, Sec/Treas
35824 West Chicago
Livonia, MI 48150

National Fishing Lure Collectors Club
  (N.F.L.C.C.)
Rich Treml, Sec/Treas
P.O. Box 1791
Dearborn, MI 48121

Bibliography

Apfelbaum, Ben. "Fish Decoys: A Native American Craft." *The Clarion*, Winter 1990, 46–49.

Apfelbaum, Ben, Eli Gottlieb, and Steven J. Michaan. *Beneath the Ice: The Art of the Spearfishing Decoy.* New York: E. P. Dutton, 1990.

Audubon Society. *Field Guide to North American Fishes, Whales, and Dolphins.* New York: Alfred A. Knopf, 1983.

Audubon Society. *Field Guide to North American Reptiles and Amphibians.* New York: Alfred A. Knopf, 1979.

Barry, Ann. "Fish Decoys Aren't Fooling Collectors." *The New York Times*, 13 August 1989.

Barton, Wayne. *Chip Carving – Techniques and Patterns.* New York: Sterling Publications, 1978.

Berry, Bob. *Fish Carving: An Introduction.* Harrisburg, PA: Stackpole Books, 1988.

Berry, Heidi L. "The Enduring Appeal of Sporting Art." *The Washington Post Washington Home*, 26 June 1986.

Bishop, Robert. "Folk Art From the Ice Fisherman." *Americana*, March/April 1978, 28–29.

Bishop, Robert, and Judith Reiter Weissman. *Folk Art: Paintings, Sculpture and Country Objects.* New York: Alfred A. Knopf, 1983.

Boesel, Jim. "Fish Decoys on Tour." *Fine Woodworking*, June 1990, 118.

Boyle, Robert H. "Gadgets Gathering Dust May Now Command Top Dollar." *Sports Illustrated*, 5 September 1988, 6–8.

Bryant, Nelson. "Hookless Lures Still Catch Notice." *The New York Times*, 18 February 1990, 6S.

Bütz, Richard. *How to Carve Wood*. Newtown, CT: Taunton Press, 1984.

Carmichael, Hoagy B. "Crafty Catches." *Art and Antiques*, Summer, 1987.

Clark, Edie. "Hooked on Fish Decoys." *Yankee*, March 1987, 92–99.

Cottle, James T. "Pike Spearing Magic." *Michigan Out-of-Doors*, February 1990, 48–52.

————. "How to Carve Fish Decoys." *Michigan Out-of-Doors*, January 1988, 33–35.

Curtis, Brian. *The Life Story of the Fish: His Moral and Manners*. New York: Dover Publications, Inc., 1961.

Dewhurst, C. Kurt, and Marsha MacDowell. "Fine Foolers of Fish." *Michigan Natural Resources Magazine*, September/October 1987, 38–43.

Dolan, Tom. *Know Your Fish*. The Hearst Corporation, 1980.

Forsthoffer, J. P. "Fish Decoys Are Luring Folk Art Buyers." *Antique Monthly*, May 1988.

Foshee, Rufus. "Fishing In Foul Waters." *Antiques Journal*, April 1990, 6.

Fritz, Ronald T. *Michigan's Master Carver Oscar Peterson 1887–1951*. Boulder Junction, WI: Aardvark Publications, Inc., 1987.

Gage, Margorie E. "Decoys Resurface." *Country Living*, April 1990, 15.

"Hooked on Lures." *Country Living*, July 1985, 43.

Hothem, Lar. "Fishing Decoys: Deceptive Collectibles." *The Antiques Journal*, April 1980.

Hubbs, Carl L., and Karl F. Lagler. *Fishes of the Great Lakes Region*. Bloomfield Hills, MI: The Cranbrook Press, 1947.

Ketchum, William C. Jr. "Delightful Deceptions." *Country Home*, February 1986, 83–87.

Kimball, Art, and Brad Kimball. *Fish Decoys of the Lac du Flambeau Ojibway*. Boulder Junction, WI: Aardvark Publications, Inc., 1988.

Kimball, Art, Brad Kimball, and Scott Kimball. *The Fish Decoy*. Boulder Junction, WI: Aardvark Publications, Inc., 1986.

————. *The Fish Decoy*. Vol. II. Boulder Junction, WI: Aardvark Publications, 1987.

MacDowell, Marsha, and C. Kurt Dewhurst. "Oscar Peterson." *Michigan Natural Resources Magazine*. November/December 1982, 58–63.

McClane, A. J. *McClane's Field Guide to Fresh Water Fishes of North America*. New York: Holt, Rinehart and Winston, 1974.

Meyerson, Howard. "Master Craftsman." *The Grand Rapids Press*, 4 February 1989, C8.

Migdalski, Edward C., and George S. Fichter. *The Fresh and Salt Water Fishes of the World*. New York: Greenwich House, 1983.

"Oliver's High Rollers Fishing Auction." *Antiques and the Arts Weekly*, 10 March 1989, 129.

Peterson, Kenneth L. "Bud Stewart: Michigan's Legendary Baitmaker." *Michigan Sportsman*, April 1985, 46–48.

Phillips, Angus. "Cottle Carves a Niche for Himself in Art World with Fish Decoys." *Washington Post*, 25 March 1990, B15.

———. "Lure of the Soo." *The Grand Rapids Press*, 9 March 1986, A21–22.

———. "Spearing in the Heart of the 'Soo'." *The Washington Post*, 5 February 1986, D3.

Rosenbaum, Seth. "American Fishing Lures and Fish Decoys." *Country Living*, July 1985.

Schroeder, Roger, and Paul McCarthy. *Woodcarving Illustrated*. Harrisburg, PA: Stackpole Books, 1983.

"Special Programs Highlight Fish Decoy Exhibition." *Antiques and the Arts Weekly*, 23 February 1990, 54.

Struck, Doug. "The Joy of Sitting Motionless, Staring at a Hole in a Frozen Lake." *The Baltimore Sun*, 17 January 1988.

"These Fish Are Keepers." *Time*, 26 February 1990, 55.

Thomas, Richard. *Metalsmithing for the Artist-Craftsman*. Radnor, PA: Chilton Book Company, 1960.

Utz, Gene. "Art-ful Deceivers." *Antiques Journal*, April 1990.

———. "Buying the Best at Brimfield." *Antiques Journal*, July 1989.

Zabar, Lori Segal. "A Collector's Guide to Fish Decoys." *The Clarion*, Fall 1986, 25–29.

OTHER CARVING AND WOODWORKING BOOKS FROM STACKPOLE:

Making Decoys the Century-Old Way, by Grayson Chesser and Curtis J. Badger. How to make the simple yet functional working decoys of yesteryear, with detailed painting instructions and 55 patterns of 11 species of ducks and geese. $24.95 hardcover.

Fish Carving: An Introduction, by Bob Berry. The emphasis is on composition, detail, and the finer points of achieving believable color for five North American freshwater fish, plus one saltwater-reef carving of lionfish and angelfish. $24.95 hardcover.

Folk Art Weather Vanes: Authentic American Patterns for Wood and Metal, by John A. Nelson. The 68 weather vane patterns are modeled on original folk art masterpieces. The author gives complete instructions for mounting the vane and offers a photographic history of American weather vanes. $16.95 paperback.

Decorative Decoy Designs: Dabbling and Whistling Ducks and *Decorative Decoy Designs: Diving Ducks*, by Bruce Burk. Each volume contains life-size color patterns, full-color reference photos, and detailed paint-mixing instructions, to help the carver achieve greater artistry and realism. $49.95 each, spiral bound.

Waterfowl Carving with J.D. Sprankle, by Roger Schroeder and James D. Sprankle. A fully illustrated reference to carving and painting 25 decorative ducks, this book includes patterns and step-by-step photographs. $39.95 hardcover.

To order books, call 1-800-READ-NOW, toll free.